OneNote User Guide

The Definitive Guide to Learn the Essentials of OneNote in No Time

2nd Edition

Hillary Benson

information is without contract or any type of guarantee assurance.

The trademarks that are used are without any consent, and the publication of the trademark is without permission or backing by the trademark owner. All trademarks and brands within this book are for clarifying purposes only and are the owned by the owners themselves, not affiliated with this document.

Contents

Introduction

The dawn of the information age spelt doom for the traditional notebook. With hundreds of programs and applications on the market today that will assist people to take down all the information they need, it is no wonder that people have stopped carrying notepads to lectures, seminars and meetings. Everyone from the large corporate conglomerate to the 1st grade student in elementary school is using some form of software to capture all the information they need, and of all the programs that there are on the market, Microsoft's OneNote is one of the best at capturing, manipulating and storing your information.

OneNote has been on the market for over a decade now, and it has been part of the Microsoft Office suite for some time as well.However, it isa program thatis discussed only by people who have experienced it, and its popularity outside the circles of those who use it requires improvement. This is surprising considering just how much you can do with the program.

OneNote is more than just a note taker, it is also a planner that is able to capture text, images, video, and audio notes, and retrieve them at the touch of a button. Its compatibility with many of the devices that are on the market today is impressive and means that you can work with it virtually anywhere.

This manual will serve to introduce you to the world of OneNote, and will give you a preview of some of the things that are possible with this powerful program.

Chapter 1:
OneNote Overview

OneNote is one of the most powerful note-taking softwares on the market today. The program allows users some of the advantages of a word processor, such as the ability to enter text, create tables, and insert pictures. However, unlike most word processors, OneNote users can also add audio and video data to their notes, allowing them to complement their written word with audio/visual data.

OneNote is designed to look like a digital notebook, and in that respect, the designers really got it right. In keeping with the notebook theme, Microsoft OneNote allows users to use virtually ANY part of the page to insert their information, and they can do this by just clicking on an area on the page. Do you want to write outside the margin? You can do that. Do you want to move to the top of the page and write something else? You can do that too. Do you want to just use it like a standard word processor? No one is going to stop you.

The data entry methods for this program are seemingly endless, and that is something that you want from any note taking software in the world we live in, where you never know what format the data you are receiving is going to be.

However, data entry is not the only place where OneNote is beating the competition. For those people who love being organized, this program will be a dream come true as it is insanely easy to arrange your work. The different pages within the program are organized into colored sections, just the way you would have colored tabs within some notebooks, and all these different pages are accessible with just one click of the mouse. Information in OneNote is written into pages, which can be assigned different colors and organized into sections. This collection of pages and sections makes up a notebook, which can be described as the digital equivalent of a tabbed ring binder.

OneNote was originally meant to work on laptops and desktop PCs, but with the passage of time and the evolution of technology, it can now work on virtually any system. Different features have been added to the program over the years to make it easier to work with on tablets and smartphones. This allows users to access the program in places where laptop computers may not be the ideal piece of equipment to use. It also allows users that have stylus enabled smartphones and tablets to literally write information into the program, making it easier to gather information and take down notes when the need arises.

OneNote is also makes gathering information easier by allowing the user to search through and index images and audio files to gain additional information. For instance, if an image has text information that is embedded within the file, OneNote can search for it and find it and display it as text on the screen. It also searches through audio files phonetically, allowing the user to save time when it comes to searching through an audio file. Perhaps one of its most useful features is enabling a user to play an audio file while they are reading notes taken during the recording. This is a very useful feature for anyone to have, however, it is even more useful to people like students and researchers who may need to use this feature to better make sense of the work that they are doing.

OneNote has one of the best multi-user features that you can find in an application today. With this feature, it is possible for anyone with access to make changes to your work. This may seem to be a feature most people would not like to have, until you think about all the professionals and students that have some form of group project that they need to complete.

With OneNote, these projects can be simplified tenfold as now all the concerned parties can have access to the information as it is being compiled, rather than having to wait for a meeting where the whole group sits down and makes presentations. The editing of the document can be done at all times, whether the user is online or offline. Notebooks can also be edited simultaneously, allowing more than one user to make changes to the notebook at the same time. This allows users to use OneNote as a sort of digital whiteboard, and also allows users to trade ideas in real time, which allows them to produce the highest quality work that they can in a very short amount of time.

However, perhaps OneNote's best feature is its save feature. Many people who are new to one note have searched the application looking for a save button. However, there is none. Instead, OneNote saves your work onto the OneDrive cloud or a network computer automatically, thereby eliminating the need for you to save every five minutes. This feature is brilliant, as it allows you to concentrate fully on your work, rather than have to remember to save your work at every other turn.

Because OneNote is part of the Microsoft Office Suite, it is compatible with all the other Office Suite programs. You can transfer your work to Word, or Excel and continue it there, especially if you are looking to publish the work that you have done. OneNote was never optimized for publishing works and many of its features actually hint at that fact. For instance, OneNote pages can be ridiculously large, unlike most word processing programs that will give you a specific range of page sizes that you can work with.

Another thing is that there is no set layout or structure to a page on OneNote. This is in stark contrast to word processing software, which always contain some layout or arrangement on a page. Also, a user can load images into a notebook without having to worry about the quality of the photo, as quality is never reduced. Many word processing programs will reduce the quality of the images that are imported into it, usually to save on size and CPU power. However, with OneNote, all the images that are loaded into it retain their original quality. This is unique attribute to have amongst most other word processing and note taking programs, and it is sure to begin a trend that others will have to follow.

As much as there is no specific layout or structure that is prevalent in OneNote, it does come with a whole range of templates that you can choose from. These templates are designed primarily for the user to save time, as within them there are different features already preprogrammed into the notebooks such as to-do lists, calendars and planners, and forms that you can customize.

The program comes with a large number of templates already available for you to use in its library. However, there are also various templates available for download online at the OneNote website and on the Microsoft Office website. Built in templates may be modified to fit your needs, on the other hand, to have a truly personalized experience, you could choose to create your own template design from any of your notebook pages. This is a very useful feature, and it shall be covered in greater detail in subsequent chapters.

Before you get started with OneNote, you will need to open a Microsoft account if you do not have one, so that the program can save your work onto the OneDrive cloud. When you first install OneNote, it will offer you a step-by-step guide on how to do this, and it will only take you a couple of minutes to complete. Once it has completed, you will be able to open the program and begin editing.

In the following chapter, you shall be given an introduction to some of OneNote's basic features, and you will be introduced to some of the changes that were made to the program in the latest version.

Chapter 2:
The OneNote Layout

Microsoft OneNote has some of the best, most helpful features of all note taking and planning programs. In this section, you shall be introduced to some of the basic features of OneNote, such as how to create a page and a notebook, so that you may better understand the program and be able to begin using it to its full potential.

OneNote Layout

Before we get started on some of the basic tasks that OneNote can carry out, it is important to understand the layout of the OneNote application. OneNote 2016 is very similar in appearance to its predecessor, but there are a few minor changes that you may have to get used to.

At the top left-hand corner of the screen is the Quick Access Toolbar. This is where all the most used commands are housed, such as save, open file and undo features. Directly below that are the Ribbon tabs, which allow you to explore the different tools that are available for you to use in OneNote. One of the changes made to the Ribbon tabs is the addition of a contextual command tab. This tab allows you to select any section of a table or recording to reveal additional features that can be used to modify the table or recording. The ribbon can be hidden from the display by clicking on the pin icon on the extreme right-hand corner of the ribbon display. Clicking the pin icon again brings the ribbon back into view.

In the top right-hand corner is the help icon, which gives users a basic overview of how to use one note, as well as giving you different tips and tricks to make your work easier. Below this is the online login button that allows you to login to the Microsoft servers. Logging into the Microsoft servers allows you to change the settings for your profile, as well as share your work with others so that they may edit or view your notebooks.

On the left-hand side of the screen is the notebooks list column. This displays a list of the recently opened notebooks, and allows you to switch between them at the click of a button. This column also has a pin icon to hide or reveal the contents of the list. The main page dominates the center of the screen like the other Microsoft Office applications. It is in this page that you will enter your information. Information is entered into pages via note containers. These containers can be resized to fit the page by dragging the edges, or they can be moved by left clicking the gripper on the left of the note. Right clicking on the gripper opens a drop down menu that gives you access to additional features.

Above the page on the left hand corner are the different tabs that separate different sections of the notebook. As was mentioned earlier, different tabs can be assigned different colors for ease of access.

The right-hand side of the screen is dominated by the notebook page column. This column allows you to switch between the pages of the notebook you are editing. It also contains an add page button at the top of the column that gives you a shortcut to create a new page. Just above the notebook page column is the search bar that allows you to find anything within the notebook, and all the other notebooks that have been saved in your cloud account, and gives you a simple way to navigate between the pages.

Chapter 3:
Pages, Sections, Notes and Quick Notes

Creating new pages, sections and notes on OneNote is a very easy and straightforward procedure. To create a new page, simply click the (+) Add Page button above the notebook page column. Doing this adds a new page to the currently displayed tab. You could also right click on the desired tab to activate a drop down menu that gives you a number of options, and click on New Page.

To create a new section within the current notebook, click the plus sign on the right of the section tab. You could also click on any tab and select the New Section option. As was mentioned earlier creating a note on a page is as simple as left clicking on any section of a page. You will notice that when you do this, OneNote automatically opens a note container. As mentioned earlier, this container can be resized and moved around the page at your convenience. If you would like to write your notes instead of typing them, select the draw tab. This is also helpful if you would like to create a sketch or draw something into the program.

A Quick Note is basically the digital equivalent of a sticky note, and is unique to OneNote 2016. Unlike notes, sections and pages though, Quick Notes can be created even when OneNote is closed, and be added sorted and edited once OneNote is opened again.

To create a new Quick Note within OneNote, first click on View to display the View Ribbon, then select New Quick Note. Quick Notes can be dragged to any part of the screen, and will remain visible until they are closed, allowing you to make any references that you need to while you work. You can also open a Quick Note by pressing Windows Key (⊞) +Alt+N on your keyboard.

Closing a Quick Note does not delete the note as Quick Notes are saved automatically as with regular notes. They are saved in the unfiled notes section of your notebook, and can be accessed by opening your Notebooks list and scrolling to the bottom of the list. To create a Quick Note outside of OneNote, simply press Windows Key+N on your keyboard.

Saving Notebooks in OneNote 2016

Notebooks can be stored on your hard drive or on your OneDrive account. However, it is recommended that you store your projects on your OneDrive account so that you can access your documents anywhere.

If you would like to save on the Cloud in OneNote 2016, you have three options to chose from depending on the type of information you would like to save. Most users will want to save personal information such as assignments, grocery lists, vacation plans and financial information. These can all be stored on the standard Microsoft OneDrive account, and can be accessed only by trusted individuals who have been given the permission to do so.

For those who are using OneNote to manipulate business information there are two options. The first is to use the Microsoft OneDrive for Business platform, which allows businesses to share information on their projects with a small, select, virtual team of people. This makes it easier for companies to organize things like marketing campaigns and product launches.

The second option is to use Microsoft SharePoint Online. This would only be useful for organizations that have teams with existing SharePoint accounts. However, it is a valuable feature for those organizations that have a formal team of professionals that are tasked with duties such as creating schedules or brainstorming ideas.

Organizing your Notebooks

Despite the fact that OneNote is a note taking software, unlike traditional notebooks, OneNote lets you rearrange the sections and pages you have created into an orderly, organized notebook.

Rearranging sections, pages and notebooks is one of the easiest things to do. To rearrange specific sections, pages or notebooks within OneNote, all you have to do is drag whatever it is that you would like to move to its new location on the section bar, page list, or notebook list.

OneNote also allows you to move pages from one section to another, therefore allowing you to fine tune your sections to make sure they make perfect sense. To move a page from one section to another, drag the page tab until the pointer is hovering above the section that you would like to transfer the page to. If you hold the pointer there for a couple of seconds, the section tab will open, allowing you to drag the page to its new location.

Moving a section from one notebook to another follows the same principle. This time however, you are going to drag the section tab to the notebook list column and let it hover above the list until the list opens. Now, drag the section to the desired notebook and let it go to complete the transfer.

To delete a particular section or page of a notebook, simply right click on the desired section or page and click delete. Should you ever need to recover a section or page that was deleted from a notebook, you can find all your deleted pages and sections in the Notebook Recycle Bin, which can be found in the History tab.

Chapter 4:
Tagging and Searching Notes

A notebook in OneNote can have hundreds, if not thousands of notes. Some of these notes will be extremely important, while others may be insignificant and not really carry any importance to the overall work. Different notes may also be about totally different things. For instance, if you have a notebook that deals with groceries, and you have organized it in such a way that every room in the house has its own section, then that means that the notes that are in the kitchen section are going to be completely different from the section on the bathroom. To differentiate and prioritize the notes in each section, you could tag them. There is no limit to what you can tag in a note and it can be anything from a single line of text to a whole paragraph.

To tag the text in a note, first select the text that you would like to tag. Under the Home tab, the tag button is on the right of the screen. Click on the icon for the tag that you would like to apply to the highlighted text to tag it. For instance if you have text that asks a very significant question that you will need to remember to answer at a later date, you could click on the purple Question icon. If you cannot find the tag that you are looking for, scroll down through the tags gallery using the arrows that appear there.

Please note that the first 9 tags in OneNote have shortcuts going from CTRL+1 to CTRL+9. This is because these are some of the most frequently used tags. Therefore, rather than having to access the tags menu every single time you want to use one of those tags, for instance the To Do tag, you can just use the keyboard shortcut (in this case CTRL+1) to tag the highlighted text.

To remove a tag that you have no more use for, click on the home tab and go to the tags gallery once again. Click on the down arrow that appears at the bottom of the box. A drop down menu should open that gives you various options, one of which will be remove tag.

An alternative way to remove a tag would be to highlight the tagged information, right-click it, and select remove tag from the drop-down menu. To remove multiple tags, first select all the text that has tags that you do not need anymore and press CTRL+0 (Zero) on your keyboard.

Searching Notes

One of the best features in OneNote is the search feature. It is extremely convenient because it allows you to search all the available notebooks in your archives, not just the one that you are editing. This means that you can start using the program immediately, and not have to worry about where you placed different notes, as OneNote will find them for you instantly.

To search for text within your notes, enter the search keywords in the search box in the right had corner of the screen. Your search results will be displayed in a window that opens below the search bar. Selecting a result will take you to the page which contains the note that has your keywords. You will notice that on the page, all the text that contains your keywords had been highlighted.

You can also search for text that is embedded within pictures, as well as note text. To search for text within images, you need to activate the Text recognition in pictures option. This can be found if you click on File > Options > Advanced. Underneath Text recognition in pictures there shall be a checkbox labeled

"Disable Text Recognition in Pictures". Select or clear the checkbox according to your needs.

If you are searching for tagged notes, rather than searching for particular keywords within the note, you can search for the tags themselves. To do this, select the Home tab, and under the Tags group, select Find Tags. A pane will open on the right side of the window labeled Tags Summary. This window will display all the tagged notes in the notebook, allowing you to easily select the note that you need.

OneNote also has the ability to search audio and Video recordings for words as well. However, like with the text recognition in pictures, this feature has to be turned on. To do so, select File > Options > Audio & Video. Depending on what you wish to do, check or clear the "Enable searching audio and video recordings for words" checkbox.

Saving to Other Formats

Like many of Microsoft's products, One Note allows you to save your documents and notes in a different format. This is especially useful if you have a notebook that you would like to share with someone who does not have One Note, or with someone who has an older version of the program. If you would like to save your work in another format, click on File > Save As, then follow the steps that appear. Finally, select the format of the file that is to be saved, for instance, Word 97-2003 document (.doc), and save the document in the selected location.

You can save notebooks as word documents, PDF files, XPS files, or HTML web pages that you can then post online.

These are just some of the basic features, however, OneNote can do a whole lot more than just create notes and search for data within those notes. It is some of these functions that we shall be looking at in the next chapter.

Chapter 5:
Advanced Features

OneNote has some impressive features for those who have gotten a handle of the basics and are ready to really start using the program to its full potential. In this chapter, we shall be looking at some of those features, and how they can help you to improve the quality of your work.

Creating a Section Group by Merging Multiple Sections

While you can group different pages into a section, sometimes it would be beneficial to have sections that are related to each other falling under the same group. This is very helpful, especially when you have a notebook that is so large that the sections tab will no longer display all of the sections in the book on the screen. Should you want to ensure that you can navigate easily and efficiently regardless of the size of your notebook, then this is a brilliant task to learn how to use.

To group the different sections together first open a Notebook that has a minimum of two sections. Once the notebook has opened, right click on any one of the section tabs, and in the drop down menu, select New Section Group. Enter the name of the group and press enter to save it. The group tab should open next to the + sign on the right of all the other section tabs.

Now that you have the group open, adding sections to the group is as simple as a dragging the tab of an existing section to the section group tab to transfer it to that section group. If your section group has multiple levels, you will need to press the green arrow on the right side of the notebook to go back up one level.

Creating a Subpages

Subpages are usually created to help group pages that are closely related to each other. Visually, the only difference between a page and a subpage is that in a subpage, the page's tab is indented, whereas with proper pages, this indentation does not exist. Creating a Subpage is as easy as creating a standard page, however, to create a Subpage there need to be at least two pages open within the book. One page will act as your main page, while the other one will act as your subpage.

To create the Subpage, drag the page that is on the right side of the page tab across the page to the right edge of the screen, until the title becomes indented. Should you want to make the Subpage a main page again, all you have to do is drag the page to the right to make it whole again. However, you could also move the page to the left to indent it even further.

You can hide the contents of a subpage, and indeed the subpage itself, by collapsing one of the main pages. This hides all the levels of subpages that are present under the main page. However, they can also be hidden by clicking on the chevron on the right side of the page tab. This Chevron means that the page has sub pages, and when the chevron is clicked on, lines showing the different subpages that the page contains appear under the page tab.

If you would like to move a page that has subpages under it, just move it like it were a normal page and the subpages will move with it, as long as they are collapsed. However, if you would like to move a subpage alone, you will have to convert it back into a page by dragging it left, and then move the page to its new location.

Obtaining Text from Pictures and Printouts

By far one of the best features on OneNote, the ability to obtain texts from pictures and printouts is extremely useful. The new update of OneNote now supports OCR (Optical Character Recognition), meaning that as long as it can make out the text in a picture or printout, it can read it and copy it into your notes. Once copied, the text can then be edited, which is a wonderful thing for students and people who work in the corporate world who are always getting printouts to read. It is also a great way to get information off flyers and business cards.

It is important to remember that the quality of the picture will determine the accuracy of the OCR tool. If the image is of low quality, or too grainy, it may be interpreted the wrong way by the program. For this reason, it is always advised that you look through the text once it has been grabbed from the image to make sure that it was translated accurately.

To obtain text from an image that you have added into OneNote already, first right click on the picture. Next choose the Copy Text from Picture option, and position the cursor in the area you would like the text to be pasted to.

If you would like to obtain text from a print out with more than one page, you first have to right click on the image of the print out and select one of the following options:

- Either Copy Text from this Page of the Printout or

- Copy Text from All the Pages of the Printout.

In the first option, the program will grab text form only the page or image that is shown or highlighted. However, with the second option, the program will grab text from all the images or pages that are present. Once you have made your selection, position the cursor in the area you would like to paste the information to and right-click.

Recording Audio and Video

Placing and video in One Note is easier than it first appears, and you can even ensure that you know when the audio was recorded by attaching a time stamp to it. One Note will also make the title of the recording searchable so that you can find it easily in the document.

To record audio or video in One Note, first click on the insert tab then select record audio or record video. An audio and video recording tab should appear on the screen, with a timestamped icon giving the date and time that the recording is being made. You must remember that the icon that pops up with the timestamp will be the same as your default audio and video player icon. For instance, if you are using VLC media player, the icon will be the default VLC player striped cone, if you are using iTunes, it will be the iTunes logo.

If you are recording video into one of your notes, a live feed will display in a pop up window as you make the recording so that you can have a preview of what the video will look like. While you are recording, you have the ability to pause or stop the recording by clicking on the pause and stop icons that pop up on the screen.

Once you have completed the recording, you can right click on the video or audio icon and select "rename" to rename the file.

This will help you customize your note even more, and add a title to the video that is more relevant to the note that you are composing.

Replaying the video once it has been recorded is also very simple. All you have to do is double click on the audio or video icon and use the audio and video playback tab to control how the video plays. During playback, you can choose to rewind or fast forward the track or video by either 1 second or 10 minutes, depending on the length of the audio or video.

Checking Spelling

One Note allows users to add unlimited amounts of text to different notebooks. This is one reason why it is so important to make sure that all the text has been spelt correctly. Just like other Microsoft applications, One Note comes with an autocorrect feature that fixes common errors in your typing as you type. However, if you would like run a full spell check in the program that is also very possible.

To run a full spell check, first click on the review tab in a particular subpage, and click on the spelling icon. Doing this should open a pane on the right side of the page. Each word identified by the spell checker can be ignored, or changed depending on the suggestions given by the program. Once the spell checking is complete, click OK on the box that pops up and the spelling pane should close.

One Note can also correct any math that you input into it if it notices any common errors. To turn on the Math Autocorrect function, all you have to do is click on file, then options, then proofing, and select Autocorrect Options. Click on the Math

Autocorrect tab and check the box next to Replace text as you type.

Converting Handwriting to Text

One of the best features in One Note is its ability to convert If you are one of those people that uses a tablet PC or if you have a tablet attached to your computer, you can draw or write straight into One Note. If you do not have a tablet you can still draw or write using your mouse or trackpad.

To input handwriting or a drawing into One Note, first attach the tablet and pen to your computer if you have them. Next, open a new drawing and select the 0.5 mm black pen (or the thickness of your choice). Write down what you would like the program to interpret for you, and using the Lasso Select tool, select the text you have just written. Then, go to the draw tab in the convert group and click the Ink to Text button. Should any errors arise during the conversion, you can correct them by clicking on the Select and Type button at the top of the page. If you have written down a math problem, rather than click on Ink to Text, you can click on Ink to Math instead, and the information you have entered will be converted into a mathematical expression.

Should you decide to use the default Pen Mode, you will be able to create both handwriting and drawings. However, there are other modes you can use if you would like to create either a drawing or a handwriting entry, such as a Create Drawings Only mode, Create Handwriting Only. You could even use the Use Pen as Pointer mode to use the pen as a pointer during a presentation.

Chapter 6:
OneNote and The Internet

Sharing Notebooks Online

Sharing notebooks on the cloud is a great way to get others involved in the work you are doing. It is also one of the easiest ways to get work done if you are working as a team as each team member will be able to access the work from wherever they are. It also allows the different team members to work on the same thing simultaneously, and track the changes that each person makes in near real time. The notes are updated every few minutes, allowing all the members of the team up to the minute updates of what all the other members are doing.

If you are editing a note as your team members are viewing it online, they will be able to see all the changes you are making as you make the, and should they change anything, you will be able to see the changes that they make.

Depending on where you saved the document, there are different ways you can shareit to the cloud. For instance, if you saved the notebook on the OneNote desktop program you will need to follow this procedure.

First, open the notebook that you would like to share, and in the menu bar click File > Share. When you do this, you will be given two options, Share with People or Share with meeting.

Should you select Share with meeting, you will have to select Share with Meeting again, and choose a meeting. Alternatively, you could start a new Skype for business meeting and share the notebook there.

If you selected Share with People, you will be supplied with a form where you can enter the names and addresses of the people you would like to share the notebook with. Once you have done that, just click share and the document will be on the cloud.

If you are sharing the notebook from OneDrive, OneDrive for Business or SharePoint Online, then the procedure you follow will be slightly different.

You will begin as you did before by opening the notebook that you would like to share and clicking File > Share. You will then select Share with People, and enter the names and/or email addresses of the people that will be receiving the notebook, and click share.

If you have a notebook that is already on the cloud, you do not need to open it. All you need to do is locate the notebook and click on the ellipsis (...) next to the notebook that you would like to share. When the menu opens, select share and enter the names and/or email addresses of the individuals that shall be receiving the notebook.

If you are sharing to SharePoint Online, you must ensure that all your team members have access to the service, as those without access will not be able to view shared content.

It is also important to note that you cannot share part of a notebook, for instance just a section or a page, you must share the WHOLE NOTEBOOK. However, you are able to set a password to some of the sections of the notebook to restrict access to those sections. If you would like to share just one page or a notebook, click on Home > Email Page. This option will allow you to send a snapshot of whatever you are working on in the program.

Once you have shared the notebook and your team has started to work on it, you and your other team members will have the ability to keep track of the changes that were made by different team members. This is made easy by a feature in OneNote that shows the changes that were made in the document by highlighting the text in bold characters, and placing the initials of the person who made those changes next to them. However, if that is not enough you can get an even more comprehensive look of the changes that were made by using the history tab.

The History Tab

The History tab is used to give the author and members of a team an overview of the changes that were made to a particular notebook, and the identity of the person who made those changes. The different buttons on the history tab include:

1. Next Unread – this moves the user on to the next unread section of the notebook. If this button is not accessible then it means that the notebook has been read in its entirety.

2. Mark as Read – This button is used to narrow down unread content. As the name suggests, it marks sections in the notebook that have been read to show that they have already been analyzed.

3. Recent Edits – This button shows all the modifications that were made to the document over a specific time period

4. Find By Author – This button searches the document for changes made by a specific author.

5. Hide Authors – As the name suggests, when this button is pressed, the authors of the notebook are either hidden or displayed.

6. Page Versions – This button allows the author to browse through older versions of the selected page.

7. Notebook Recycle Bin – This is where all the deleted notes, sections, and pages go. If you ever need to restore a deleted page, section, or note this is where you will find it.

Taking Notes During an Online Meeting

The fact that OneNote is fully integrated with Microsoft Outlook and Skype for Business means that you can easily take notes in any one of these programs and share them with anyone else.

If you are using Microsoft Outlook for the meeting before you start taking notes you have to open the Outlook calendar and select the meeting that you want to take notes on. Next, open the meeting ribbon and open the Meeting Notes Dialogue box. In this dialogue box you will have two options, one is to share your meeting notes with the rest of the people taking part in the meeting, or to take notes for yourself.

If you would like to share your notes with the rest of the meeting then all you have to do is select Share notes with the meeting. If you want to take your own notes choose Take notes on your own.

A Choose Notes to Share with Meeting dialogue box should appear when you select Take notes on your own. When it does, select a section and a page to record the new notes, then select

OK. Microsoft OneNote links all the pages that are used during the meeting to the Outlook Appointment. This means that you are always able to access the notes and other details from that meeting as they are all kept in a central location.

If you do find yourself in a meeting where it is not necessary for you to share the notes that you are recording, you could open the Home tab and choose Meeting Details.

Using OneNote Add-Ins

OneNote has a number of additional programs that you can use to help make your experience with the program better. These programs help you do things like format your content, print documents, capture data from whiteboards and even share team notebooks. Listed below are just some of the popular add-ins that are available for OneNote, and a short description of their different functions within the program.

1. **Onetastic**

Onetastic is one of the most versatile of all the add-ins that are available for one note. Apart from allowing users to create custom styles for their notebooks, it also displays content in a calendar. Its best feature has to be the Macro functionality, which unlocks a whole new world of possibilities within OneNote. For instance users can now create features like Find and Replace, Daily Journal View and Author Information Removal. There are currently over 180 different macros available on the Onetastic website, and more are bound to be unveiled as people find more ways to simplify their OneNote experience. The best part about it all is that Onetastic and its Macros are absolutely free

2. **Office Lens**

This is an add-in that is most useful on the mobile and tablet platforms. It allows the camera's on these devices to take all sorts of images, including those of business cards, white boards, and documents, and saves them directly into OneNote. Once the images are saved, they can be loaded into OneNote to have the data in them translated by the OCR.

3. **Clip to OneNote**

This add-in by OneNote Gem Add-Ins is a brilliant third party application for use with web browsers. It is designed to send the active web page in a web browser as a single image to OneNote's Quick Notes section. It supports all the major browsers, including Internet Explorer, Mozilla Firefox, Google Chrome, Opera, and Safari.

Chapter 7:
One Note for Education

One Note is one of the most powerful tools that educators, teachers and students have at their disposal. In fact, it is such a versatile tool that Microsoft themselves created an entire website that is dedicated to One Note and Education, as well special tools that teachers and students can use called the One Note Class Notebook and the One Note Staff Notebook.

These tools allow teachers and students alike to stay organized and work together easier to be able to achieve the goals for the curriculum they are studying or teaching. It also allows teachers to work together to make planning and executing the curriculum easier for them.

The sections that One Note offers allows teachers to section their notes so that they know when different activities should take place, for instance, meetings such as staff meetings, department meetings, and PTA meetings, and all the notes that go along with those meetings. One Note's ability to sync with Microsoft Outlook also allows teachers to have finer control of the notes that you create, and allows them to add meetings to their One Note notebooks easily, including the date, time and people who shall be attending the meeting. If the notebook that the teacher is modifying uses a specific template, the information imported from Microsoft Outlook will automatically adopt the same template, meaning that users will not have to worry about modifying information once it has been imported.

Another thing that teachers will find useful is One Notes ability to gather information from different places while keeping the information from the sources. For instance, teachers who are researching on a particular subject may find interesting websites that they can use in class. The information from these websites can be saved as a screenshot that can then be used in their classroom presentations in class. The screenshot, once imported to one note, will have all the information relating to the source that the teacher needs, including the page URL and information on the website that it was taken from.

There are many teachers out there that also use One Note to organize their to-do lists for different tasks, including administrative and classroom tasks and activities. Once the tasks have been completed you can tick them off just like a normal to-do list, and because they are automatically saved on to the cloud, you can modify them from anywhere, and on any device that has access to the internet.

Important notes and activities can be grouped together using the tags summary, allowing teachers to have easy access to important items, questions and to do lists all in one place. Should the information not have been tagged, the One Note search engine is so powerful that it will be able to find the information they are looking for regardless of how the notebook is organized.

Teachers can also create pages for different students, or groups of students, in each of their classes. By doing this, they can then file all the students information, including contact information, disciplinary records and grades in one place. One Note integration with Microsoft Outlook also makes it easier for teachers to import student information into One Note, and allows them to update information quickly and easily when the need arises. Even when the teachers are busy carrying out other duties, they can use One Note to record their thoughts and ideas by creating Quick Notes.

Creating Fun and Interactive Classes using One Note

Teaching these days has become much more demanding thanks to the increased demand for interesting interactive classes. Teachers can no longer enter a classroom and assume that they will be able to teach effectively using only a text book and a few PowerPoint slides. This is one of the reasons why One Note is such a powerful tool for teachers, it allows them to create interesting, interactive classes that every student will enjoy. The best part of the interactive lessons is that they can be created in such a way that the students will be able to complete them by themselves at a later date.

Lessons can be created with custom audio introductions that help to explain the objectives of the lesson and the expected outcomes of the lesson. One Note's ability to create hyperlinks automatically means that you can attach links to articles, audio, video among other links to the lesson, allowing students to access the additional information that they need easily.

Teachers are also able to link assignments to the lesson. For instance, if you have an assignment that you have prepared on One Note already, all you need to do is link the assignment to the lesson note and students will be able to access and complete the assignment. Once they have completed their homework, One Note allows teachers to grade the assignments in the application, and teachers can even add audio commentary to the assignment to further explain where a student went wrong, or to add praise to work that was well done. An added advantage of doing this is that the comments added can be linked to the audio recordings that you create automatically thanks to the timestamp feature.

Creating assignments on One Note becomes even more important for those lessons that involve practical skills such as music, geography and foreign languages. For instance, if you are a music teacher, you can add audio samples to a particular assignment to test your students' ability to recognize certain tunes or progressions. You could also test your students' knowledge of different geographical features using the different drawing tools provided by the application. Foreign language classes can be made even more interactive by having the teacher create pronunciation assignments that the students complete by following different audio files to test their skills. The teacher could then add their comments of how to improve their pronunciation while they are grading the assignment.

Collaborating with Teachers and Students using the One Note Class Notebook App

Teachers need to collaborate with each other and their students, to ensure that their students gain the best education possible. This is especially important when it comes to class projects, creating assignments, and providing feedback concerning a student's performance. The One Note Class Notebook allows teachers to create notebooks that have preset permissions that have been specially designed to be used in the classroom and in learning environments, whether they are in schools or colleges.

To create a class notebook, you first have to enter Microsoft Office 365, and click on the One Note Class Notebook. You will then be able to create a new Notebook, and enter the name of the class that you are teaching.

Once the class notebook opens, you will realize that it has been partitioned into three different "spaces", these are:

- **The collaboration space** – this space allows teachers and students alike to edit the information that is in the note. This is especially useful for group work and class projects.

- **The content library** – this space allows teachers to modify the information in the note, however, it only allows students to view the information and copy the contents if they feel the need to do so. This space is best utilized for giving out tests, assignments and course materials that students may need.

- **Student notebooks** – these are the students own space where they can work without worrying about other students viewing their work. Teachers and instructors will be able to view every student notebook in their class, and edit the information in the notebook to help improve the student's work. However, no other students will be able to access a private student notebook that is not their own.Every student notebook that you create comes with a few default sections. However, you could modify these sections by adding or removing some of the sections that were suggested.

Adding students to a class is easy, and can be done by manually entering the different students in the class, or by importing a group from Azure Active Directory or Office 365. Should the members of the group change after the notebook has been created, you can modify the group in the One Note Class Notebook app by clicking on Add or Remove Students.

Once you are done editing or creating your class notebook, you are provided with a preview to ensure that you have created a notebook that will benefit yourself and your students. The preview has two different views, one that only the teacher will be able to see, and another that is exclusively for the student.

Once the notebook has been created, teachers are supplied with a link that they can send to the students so that they can access their notebooks. This link can also be used to open the notebook directly, so it would be a good idea to save it somewhere if you are a teacher.

The notebook can then be edited so that it provides all the information that students' will use for that semester. The specially designated sections in the Class Notebook allow teachers to collaborate with students and share information on a convenient platform.

Modifying the teachers or students that are allowed to view the notebook is simple, and only requires the teacher to go to the notebook and click the add or remove students/teachers icons and follow the instructions. It is important to remember that despite the fact that an individual has been removed from the notebook, the information that they contributed to the notebook will remain, though they will no longer be able to access the notebook itself.

Once you have added or removed students or teachers from the notebook, you will be directed to a screen that shows all the modifications you have made. All you need to do to ensure that the changes are permanent is to click on the update button at the bottom of the screen. The app will then create a new link to the notebook that you can send to the new student or teacher if you chose to add individuals to the book.

Any students that use Office 365 will be sent a notification immediately a One Note Class Notebook is shared with them. For those who may not use Office 365, they could also access the Class Notebook by clicking on the "shared with me" folder in Microsoft One Drive.

Sharing Class Notebooks with other teachers is just as simple as sharing them with students, and follows the same basic procedure. You must first add teachers to the notebook by clicking on the "Add or Remove Teachers" icon, then following the steps outlined by the program, which are much the same as when you were creating a list of students. A link that you can send to teachers and other instructors will then be generated.

Perhaps the best thing about the One Note Class Notebook is that you can modify all the notebooks you create from one place. All you have to do is click or tap on the Manage Notebooks icon, and a list of all the Class Notebooks you have created will appear. You can then change the specifics of any one of the notebooks displayed without having to worry about opening a new notebook every time that you need to change a minor detail.

For instance, you can change the name of a teacher or student section, add or remove student sections, and even change the permissions of certain spaces in the notebook. For example, if you feel that your students should not be able to change the information in the collaboration space, all you have to do is click on a button and they will no longer be able to do so. Once you have made all the desired changes, you will have to click on save to update the notebook and ensure that all the changes that you have made are permanent.

Class notebooks can be used to give out and grade assignments. All you have to do is go to the content library and create a new assignment. Once the assignment has been created, students will be able to get the assignments from the content library by copying the assignment into their own notebooks. When the homework has been completed, the teacher can then grade the work by opening the student's notebook and giving comments and feedback on the assignment as described earlier.

The teacher only section group is one of the most useful things for teachers, as it allows them to set up lesson plans and assignments in the same notebook without allowing the students to see what they are doing. It also allows teachers to create content that they do not want the students to access until they feel the time is right.

Chapter 8:
One Note for Android

One Note may have been designed for use with Windows computers and laptops, but for those who would like to access the program through their mobile devices, Microsoft developed One Note for Android. This application allows users to have most of the features that One Note for Windows has, though it is a lighter, stripped down version of the original. The application was developed mainly due to the extremely small market share that Windows Phones have, and the demand that Android users had for a version of the application that could run on their devices.

For instance, the interface on One Note for Android has been designed specifically for smartphones and tablets, and works just as well as the version created for Windows Phones. The interface if very utilitarian, a fact that becomes especially obvious when you use the app on a tablet.

There are a number of major elements that make up the One Note for Android interface. These include:

1. **The Note Pane** – this pane takes up the whole screen, except for the top strip that houses the various buttons that you will need when using the app

2. **The Up Button** – the up arrow button can be found in the upper left corner of the screen, except when you are on the One Note homepage. If you tap it you will automatically be taken back to the section, note or list that you were looking at before you switched to a new page.

3. **The Command Buttons** – located in the top right corner of the screen, the command buttons are three buttons that work anywhere in One Note except for the home screen. These buttons are usually arranged in the following order:

- **Recent Notes:** The left-most button of the three, this button gives you access to notes that you have modified or created recently

- **New Note:** This button is placed in the middle of the three, and allows you to create a new blank note with your cursor in the title field.

- **Take a picture:** This button is placed on the right of the three buttons, and it allows you to take a photo with your device's camera and add it to your note.

4. **Keyboard** – immediately you tap on any note so that the cursor appears, the keyboard shall pop up from the bottom of your screen just as it does with any other Android app.

Writing Notes on One Note for Android

Just like with all the other mobile versions of One Note, such as the one for iOS, the Android version of One Note gives you access to your notes, and allows you to edit them (though with much fewer features than the desktop version) at the touch of a button.

To create a new note from anywhere on One Note for Android, all you have to do is tap on the middle button in the upper right corner of your screen. If you are in the middle of viewing a note, the new note that you create will be inserted into the section that you are viewing. However, if you are on the home screen, the new note that is created will be stored in the Unfiled Notes section of your Web or Personal notebook.

It is important that you remember that the icon will not appear at the top of the page if the cursor is in a note, therefore, you may have to tap on the back button on your device to ensure that the button actually appears at the top of your screen.

Opening notes on One Note for Android is just as simple, and only needs you to tap the note's name when you are viewing the section that it is stored in. if you would like to open a note from the home screen, you will first have to tap the name of the notebook that the note is in, then tap the name of the section it is in and finally, tap the name of the note.

List elements are hidden in One Note for Android until you need them. Accessing them is very easy, and involves you opening a note so that the buttons on the screen change. Once you are inside the note, you will see four buttons at the top of the screen. The first button is the camera button, and the next three are list element buttons. They are used to create a numbered, bulleted or check boxed list depending on your preferences.

Recording Audio on One Note For Android

Sometimes the inspiration to record audio for one of your notes will hit you while you are on the move. To help you record all those moments, One Note for Android allows you to record audio, and will even translate the audio you record to text that will be displayed in the note that is open at the time of the recording. You can record into One Note easily using the microphone button included in the keyboard of all Android Devices.

To record audio and have it translated to text, you must first open a new note and tap the area where you would usually type. Once the keyboard appears, tap on the microphone button and speak when the Speak Now prompt appears. You will notice that once you start speaking, the Speak Now prompt changes and becomes Tap to Pause.

Once you have paused the recording, you can choose to do one of two things, ether tap the screen again to continue speaking or tap the keyboard icon so that you can switch back to the standard keyboard and stop recording. As One Note will interpret your speech and translates it into text you may have to correct some errors in interpretation when you are done.

Adding Pictures to One Note for Android

These days nearly all android devices have some sort of camera, and One Note can utilize this camera to add pictures to any of the notes that you are editing. You could add pictures to a note in many different ways including:

1. **Using the Take Photo Button**: The take photo button is usually a camera icon with a lightning bolt that sits in the upper-right corner of the interface when you are not in an actual note. If you tap this icon, you will be able to takephotos for the note that you are viewing. If you tap the button while you are in any notebook, a note called Unfiled Note will be created and stored in your Web or Personal notebook. Your photo will be stored in this note until you file it in a particular notebook.

2. **The Photos Button:** The icon for the photos button is usually in the top left corner of your screen when your cursor is in a note. Tap this button to bring up a pop up window that you can use to add photos from your gallery or to take a new photo that will be stored in the note.

Capturing images and storing them in your notes is extremely easy, especially if you are already well versed with the functions of your phone's camera. You must remember that One Note does not have its own camera, and that it only borrows your device's camera to take photos. The functions of your device's camera will be dictated by the version of Android that you are using. However, there are some camera functions that may not be supported by One Note, so you have to make sure that the functions that your camera is capable of are supported by the app before you use them. At the time of writing, One Note for Android still did not support capturing and adding video to the notes that you create on the app.

If you would like to take a new photograph to add in a note page, you can use the following procedure:

1.   If you are not already in the note pane, tap it to edit it then tap the camera icon in the upper left corner of the screen. The insert menu will pop up and give you a variety of options that you can use to add images from your gallery or take a photograph

2.   Tap capture a photo and use Android's default camera to capture an image. If you do not want to take a photo after all you can always tap the X that appears on the bottom right hand corner of the screen. The bottom left hand corner will usually have a button that allows you to change the settings of your camera

3. Take a photo as you would usually do, the X will remain at the bottom of the screen, but the camera options button will be replaced by a check mark symbol.

4. Tap the X if you do not like the picture you have taken and keep taking photos until you are satisfied, then hit the check box on the bottom left of the screen. Your note will reappear with the chosen photo attached.

Adding a phot that you have already taken is just as simple, and can be done in the following ways:

1. If you are not already there, tap the note pane to edit it and tap the camera icon at the top of the screen. When the insert menu appears, add a picture from your gallery

2. Tap the add image from gallery icon, and add an image from your selected gallery, be it OneDrive or your phone's gallery. You will then be asked whether you always want to use this source or if you are using it just once, make the appropriate selection and select the photo that you would like to attach to the note. If you tapped always but would like to change the setting later on, the easiest way to do so would be to tap the Clear Data button in the One Note app in Android settings.

Managing Notebooks and Notes on One Note for Android

Despite the fact that it is a more toned down version of its desktop counterpart, you can still manage the different notebooks and notes that you create in One Note on your Android device. For instance, if you would like to delete a note, you can do so by tapping the Delete Page button in the Options Pane while you are viewing the note. However, if you would like to rename, delete or move whole sections or notebooks, you will have to access the OneDrive app or the web app version of One Note.

Settings on One Note for Android

Despite the fact that you have very few settings that you can change in One Note for Android, there are certain settings that you can change that you may find useful. Finding the Options pane on One Note is easy, as the three vertical dots that can be found in the bottom right corner of the screen are more or less universal across most Android apps. However, the buttons do change slightly depending on where you are in the app, and the menu is designed to be context sensitive, meaning that it changes depending on where you are in the app.

For instance, if you are on the Home Screen, or in a Notebook Section, the Options pane will only have three options, Sync, Sync Error, and Settings. However, if you are in a section editing pages, then the Options pane will also have a Create New Page button. Should you be viewing a note, then the Create New Page button will become a Delete Page button instead.

The purpose of the different buttons is as follows:

- **Delete page:** Deletes the page you are viewing

- **New Page:** Creates a new page in the section that you are viewing

- **Settings:** Most of the settings that you can change in One Note for Android can be found when you click this button

- **Sync:** Clicking this button will sync the current page with the notebook saved on your One Drive cloud storage space

- **Sync Error:** This only lights up when there has been an error syncing the note with One Drive. Click on the icon when it appears to gather more information on the error

Once you open the Settings menu, you will be able to modify certain things about One Note For Android. Some of the options available to you in this menu include:

- **Sync on Wi-Fi only:** by tapping this checkbox, you will be confirming that you will only be able to sync notes and notebooks with One Drive when you are connected to Wi-Fi. This will help you to conserve your mobile data.

- **Windows Live ID Account:**should you ever want to view the account that you are logged in to while using One Drive for Android this is the button you should tap. Usually, you are redirected to a window in the Android settings app, not One Note itself. In the app, there is another options button in the upper right corner of the screen that you can press to either Sync Now, Remove Account or access Help. The Help feature opens a webpage in your browser that allows you to view the help documentation that is related to your device.

- **Upgrade:** One Note for Android is usually free for the first 500 notes, after which you will not be able to edit or create any more notes until you delete some. However, if you pay a small fee, you can upgrade your One Note for Android app so that you can edit unlimited notes

- **Help:** Clicking on help opens a webpage in your default web browser that contains all the help information for your particular device.

- **Support:** Tapping on support will bring up your web browser, and load the different support forums that have been started on the Microsoft website for One Note for Android

- **Use Terms:** Tapping this will bring up a pop-up window that will display the apps terms of use

- **Privacy Statement:** Tapping on this will bring up a tab in your default web browser that will display Microsoft's privacy statement.

- **Third Party Notice:** This item will bring up a pop up window that will give you more information about any third-party technologies that you are using in Microsoft One Note for Android

- **Version:** Tapping this will give you more information on the version of One Note for Android that you are using

- **Copyright:** Tapping this option will display the copyright language for the app.

Despite the fact that it is a prominent feature in both One Note for iOS and Desktop versions of One Note, you cannot change the settings for picture quality on One Note for Android. This means that some of your photos may appear to have a lower quality than they actually do, while others will be viewed in their full scale, regardless of what you try.

There are some One Note settings that are not available from within the app itself, but are available through the device settings. To view those settings, you will have to tap the settings icon on your device and select the One Note app in the list of installed apps. Some of the options that are not available via the app but are available in your device's app menu include:

- **Force Stop:** Tapping this button allows you to stop One Note and close it if it will not close any other way. It stops all processes pertaining to the program.

- **Uninstall:** Tapping this button will uninstall the app from your device

- **Clear Data:** Tapping on this button will temporarily clear all the data that is stored on your device by the application. However, when you log in again, the data that had been cleared will be restored.

- **Clear Cache:** This button will clear all the information that One Note has stored on your system Cache. If the app is misbehaving, you can try to tap this button after you have tapped on Force Stop, then restart the app.

Chapter 9:
One Note for iOS Devices

As the first non-windows devices to receive One Note, the iPad, iPod touch and iPhone were given greater focus, and for that reason, the interfaces on these devices is much better than that on the Android version of the application. In fact, One Note for iOS is even more advanced than One Note for Windows Phone, though it still has fewer functions than One Note for Windows and even the One Note web application.

The One Note for iOS Interface

Navigating through One Note for iOS is a unique experience, as many of the cool features, animations and styles that are used have been optimized to run on Apple devices. All iOS devices, except the iPad have basically the same interface, and the only real difference between the interface on the iPad and other iOS devices is the size of the display, which makes the interface look dramatically different on the iPad.

There are two different orientations used in One Note for iPad, Landscape and Portrait. In Landscape view, you have access to a navigation bar on the left side of the screen, and the note pane is on the right. However, in portrait mode, the navigation pane disappears, and all you have is the note pane that fills the whole screen. The navigation bar is accessed via an icon on the left side of the screen.

On the iPhone and iPod Touch, each pane takes up the whole display, and the buttons are all placed at the top and bottom of the screen. Some of the main features of the interface on the One Note for iOS devices include:

- **The Note Pane:** The note pane usually takes up the whole display when in portrait, and two thirds of the screen in Landscape orientation in the iPad version. It looks like a piece of paper in a ring binder on the iPad. For the other iOS devices, the pane takes up the whole display, much like it does on the iPad in portrait orientation, just smaller. Above the note pane you can see where you are in the notebook.To change locations in the notebook or section that you are viewing, all you have to do is tap on the name of the notebook or section that you would like to view and you will be redirected straight to that section or notebook. For instance, if you would like to view a list of pages that are in a particular section, all you have to do is tap on the name of the section. If you would like to view a list of the sections in the notebook, tap on the notebook name and a list of all the sections in the notebook shall be displayed.

- **The List Pane:** This pane is where you can view a list of your notebooks, the sections contained in a notebook, and the pages that are in a section. To view an item, all you have to do is tap it and it will be displayed below all pinned items. The Recents tab creates a pin icon on the right of every item you have viewed. By tapping this icon, you can move the item to the top of the list regardless of the item that you have touched. The item that you pin next will go below the top item and so on.

- **The Back Button:** The back button appears in the upper left corner of the display on every window except the home page. The button resembles a left facing arrow, and tapping it will take you to any section, note or list that you were viewing previously. Depending on where the button will take you and where you are in the notebook, the text that accompanies the back button will change. For instance, if you are viewing notebook sections, the button will display home, however, if you are displaying a particular page in a section of a notebook, it will display the name of the notebook. It is important to remember that regardless of the text that the button displays, its primary function is a back button.

- **New Section Button:** This button appears next to the back button everywhere except on the home screen

- **View Icons/Search Button:** The bottom of the window contains three buttons that you can tap to change what you view on the display. The first changes the view of the list pane and shows you any unfiled notes that you may have, the next button displays recent notes, and the third brings up the search view.

- **Keyboard:** once you have opened a note, when you click on the pane a keyboard will appear automatically. The keyboard on iOS devices has its own functions including a check box button that you can tap to add check boxes to items that you have selected, and a bullet button that adds bullets to the selected text. It also contains a camera button that allows you to take photos to add to a note, or to add pictures to the note, and a return button that changes depending on where you are in the app. For instance, if you are trying to log in, the button will display Sign In, while if you are trying to search for something, the button will read Search rather than Return. If you would like to close the keyboard, just tap on the close keyboard button on the bottom right on of the keyboard.

Creating and Editing Notes in One Note for iOS

When it comes to creating, writing and editing notes on One Note for iOS, the process has been made as simple as possible, though you must remember that the app has fewer features than its online and desktop counterparts.

Creating a new note is simple and can be done regardless of where you are in the application. All you have to do is tap the new note icon in the upper right hand corner of the window to reveal a pop up menu with two options, Create Note (Unfiled) or Create Note in Current Section. The first choice creates a new note in your Web or Personal notebook and stores it under Unfiled Notes, while the second option creates a note in whatever section displayed at the top of the window, regardless of where you are in the application. If you are actually viewing the Web notebook's unfiled section and you click on the New Note option then the second option will be unavailable because it is basically redundant.

If you would like to open an existing note from Microsoft One Drive that is relatively simple as well. All you have to do is access the home screen and tap the name of the notebook, the name of the section, and the name of the note that you wish to access.

Adding a picture is also very simple, and can be done by tapping on the camera icon at the top of the keyboard. You will then be presented with two options:

1. **Camera:** Tapping on camera will activate your iOS device's camera, allowing you to take a picture that you can then add to your note. The camera interface is relatively easy to understand, and even has a button that can change the

camera you are using between the rear camera and the front camera. After you take your picture, two icons will appear at the bottom of the screen, the one of the left allows you to discard the photo you just took and take a new one, while the one on the right confirms that the photo you have been taken is the one that you would like to insert into the app.

2. **Photo Library:** Tapping on this option will allow you to choose an item from your device's photo library

If your device does not have a camera, then you will be presented with two different options, Saved Pictures and Photo Stream.

When it comes to renaming notes and notebooks, the procedure is much the same as with the One Note for Android App, with many of the same restrictions. This means that you can edit the name of a note, but you cannot edit the name of a section or the whole notebook without logging on to the One Note web app or desktop application. You also cannot create a new notebook in One Note for iOS.

However, you can delete notes in the iOS app using one of two procedures

1. Swipe the note item to the left in the list pane. A red delete button will appear, and if you are sure that you would like to delete the note then you can tap delete and the note will disappear.

2. Tapping the trash can icon at the top of the display will bring up a menu with an option to delete a page, if you are sure you want to delete the page tap the Delete This Page option and the note will disappear.

Searching through Notes in One Note for iOS

Searching through notes in One Note for iOS is much the same as searching through notes on the web and desktop applications, and the search feature allows you to search for single terms in the notes contained in all the different notebooks. However, due to the limited functionality of the app compared to the desktop version, you can only search for text within notes, and you cannot search for pictures or tags.

Searching for text in One Note for iOS is as simple as tapping the search button at the bottom of the screen and type the search term into the Search Notebooks field at the top of the list pane. The results of your search should appear in the list pane below the search field. Once you have found the note that you would like to edit, you can view it in the note pane by tapping it. You will not lose any of your search results when you do this as the list pane will not be affected by your tapping on the note.

Managing notebooks on One Note for iOS app has been made extremely difficult, and the only way to effectively rename, delete or move notebooks is through the One Drive app for iOS.

Configuring One Note for iOS

One Note for iOS has very few settings that you can actually modify. To change the settings that are available to you in the app, the first thing you must do is tap the settings button at the top of the home screen. The window that opens has a number of options including:

1. **Upgrade:** Like One Note for Android, One Note for iOS limits the number of notes that you can have to

500. However, you can have unlimited notes if you pay a nominal fee to upgrade the app.

2. **Sync Now:** Tapping on this item immediately syncs all notes that are programmed to sync automatically

3. **Notebook Settings:** This button allows you to choose which notebooks to sync automatically while simultaneously allowing you to choose which notebooks will be displayed on the home screen

4. **Image Size:** A feature that is notably absent from its Android counterpart, the image size setting allows you to select the size of the images that you insert into different notes

5. **Sign Out:** Tapping this button will sign you out of One Note

6. **Help and Support:** Tapping this button will open a window that gives you links to different community support forums and help documentation

7. **Terms of Service:** Tap this button if you would like to view One Note's terms of service

8. **Privacy:** Tap this button if you would like to view One Note's privacy settings

Just like with its Android counterpart, One Note for iOS has some settings that you cannot change within the app, but that you can change using your device's settings. To access these settings, tap on the settings icon on your device, and tap on the One Note icon in the settings pane. The settings that appear are outlined below:

1. **Sync on Wi-Fi Only:** This particular option ensures that notebooks will only sync with One Drive when you are within Wi-Fi range. This allows you to keep the data usage of the app to a minimum, and ensures that you do not go over your data limit.

2. **Reset Application**: This feature is especially useful when you have sync errors, or other errors that will not fix themselves regardless of how many times you restart the application. Once activated, you will have to sign yourself back in to One Note, but you will not lose any information

3. **Version**: There is nothing you can do to change this setting as it is just a description of the version of the app that you currently have installed on your device.

Managing Syncing and Images in One Note for iOS

Setting individual notes to sync automatically is something that may seem unnecessary, but is one of the most useful features of One Note for iOS, especially if they are set up so that they sync regardless of whether you can see them on the home screen or not. The steps below outline how to turn OFF automatic syncing for particular notebooks, though following the opposite of this procedure will turn ON syncing for any notes that you may have created:

1. When you are viewing the home screen, tap the settings button at the top of the screen and tap on notebook settings. A pop up window should appear

2. Tap on the on slider that is next to a notebook to turn syncing off for that particular note. Once the slider is in

the off position, you will not be able to view the notebook on the homepage, and the note will not sync automatically.

3. Close the settings pane by tapping on the settings button and then tapping the close button in the upper right hand corner of the window. Once you return to the Home screen, you will realize that the notes that you have toggled off are no longer visible, and they will not sync automatically.

Managing image settings on One Note for iOS is simple despite the fact that there are quite a few options to choose from when it comes to how you would like the app to display photos. For instance, you can choose from a wide range of image sizes when you are inserting the images to notes:

- Small sets the images to .5 megapixels

- Medium sets the images to 1 megapixel

- Large sets the images to 2 megapixels

- Actual Size will display the photo in notes at their actual sizes

- Ask me will ensure that you receive a prompt every time you try to insert an image in a note so that you can determine for yourself how large the image should be when it is being inserted into the note.

Chapter 10:
Top 10 Tips for One Note Users

There are many tips and tricks that have been outlined in this book that will make using One Note that much simpler. There are also many scenarios that have been described that show you how useful the application can be. This chapter aims to emphasize some of these points, while simultaneously give you a few tips which could make your use of the program easier.

1. Backing up Important Data

Syncing and backing up of notes and notebooks has been discussed at length in various sections of this book, but the importance of this feature needs to be emphasized one more time so that you can truly understand how useful the feature can be.

Consider this scenario, you are on your way to Europe from the West coast for a well-deserved vacation and need to catch a connecting flight in New York. However, when you arrive in New York, you realize that you have lost your hand luggage, and that it had all the information you need for your trip. However, you still have your cell phone, and you remember that your itinerary was saved in One Note, which you can access through your phone. Because of the data backup, you make it to your next plane with barely a moment to spare, but you find it, and you're on your way to Barcelona.

Another scenario where you could be saved by the backup feature on one note this, you are on your way for a job interview, but you forget to bring and review your resume to the meeting. However, you have backed everything up on One Note and you have your iPad with you. You go for the interview anyway, and when you are asked for your resume, you hand over your iPad with all the information that your future employer needs on it. You never know, you may ace the interview purely because you have your resume on an iPad.

Perhaps you were on your way for a meeting at work and you forgot to carry that report that was due today because you were more occupied with chowing down breakfast and getting out of the house as fast as you can. Now you are two hours away from home and the meeting is in an hour. Then you remember that you have the presentation on One Note and all you have to do is print out the hard copies and connect your phone to the projector and you're sorted.

The number of scenarios that One Note could help with are limitless, but the examples outlined above should be enough to show just how important the application can be.

2. You Have Access To Entire Office Documents On Your Phone At The Touch Of A Button

One Note is one of the only office apps that allows you to access documents easily on Android. Despite the fact that you may not be able to work much on your documents, you will at least be able to access and view them on your mobile device.

This feature is especially useful when you realize that saving the document as a printout on One Note rather than pasting it in to the application will allow you to view it exactly the same way you would in the original program. You may not be able to edit the documents, but you will at least be able to view them perfectly in One Note. If you have the One Drive application on your phone, you can access Word, Excel and PowerPoint documents via the appropriate web applications and actually edit the files, though you will have limited features compared to the full office applications.

3. Dictating Notes to Text

This is another feature that has been addressed in earlier chapters, but its importance cannot be emphasized. Though this feature is most useful in One Note for Android as it does not allow you to store recorded voice notes, it is a very useful option that should be seen as an added feature rather than a missing option, especially if that was your aim in the first place. This feature is especially useful for those people that have to translate a lot of dictated audio into plain text.

4. Retrieving Text from Images

This feature has been discussed at length in previous chapters, but its importance cannot be overstated, especially for those people who work with images on a regular basis. The fact that it is so easy to do is one of the best things about this feature, however, it is important to note that you have to ensure that your photograph is of the highest quality possible to ensure that the text that you are trying to grab from the image comes out as clearly as possible.

You must also ensure that the photo is not too dark or too bright, and that the font in the picture is not one of those difficult to read calligraphic fonts that are sometimes used, especially by creative individuals. However, in most cases, even if the picture is dark or the font is hard to read, you will still be able to retrieve at least some of the text, meaning you will be able to avoid most of the retyping that you need to do.

5. Taking a Screengrab and Marking it

As was mentioned previously, one of the best things about One Note is that you can take a screen shot of something using the clipping tool in the application. You can then use the pen tool in One Note to mark up the image. This is a very useful feature especially if you would like to add notes and comments to a photograph or image and share it for the world to see. For instance, if you are in the middle of developing a website and you would like to show your contributors what you would like to keep or change in the website, you can use the pen tool to note anything that you feel should be noted.

If you do not have a computer to a PC that has digital pen technology, you could always use actual text, or you could even use your mouse pointer as a pen and draw your comments if your handwriting with the mouse is good enough.

6. Marking Up Documents with a Pen

Should you be able to access a digital pen-capable PC, you will realize that marking up documents in One Note is easy. However, if you would like to ensure that you keep some of the similarities to the original document's formatting, then you will find it is easier to import a printout of the document instead of copy/pasting the contents of a page or document onto the note page.

If you have access to other Microsoft Office applications on your pen-capable PC then there are some cases where you could use the pen to mark up the documents in that app in much the same way. However, you must keep in mind that it can be trickier to do so in those apps, so it may be easier to just stick to One Note when marking up documents.

7. Copying links into Paragraphs

If you ever need to create links to specific parts of a One Note page, you can do it easily by right-clicking on the paragraph or note container that you would like to link and clicking on the Copy Link to Paragraph option. This will allow you to copy a link to your computer's clipboard, and you can then add that link to any document of your choice.

8. Searching Text In Images

This is another feature that has been addressed before but cannot be emphasized enough. The ability to search for text in images means that any image that you drop into One Note that has text in it can be discovered as long as you make the text in the image searchable. Even better, you can specify the language that the text is in so that you can find it later. This will allow you to find images quickly regardless of the language that the text in the photograph is in.

9. Docking One Note to the Desktop

If you find yourself using One Note regularly, you can make sure that it is always within easy reach by placing it beneath all your other open windows. This will ensure that you do not always have to select it from the taskbar, and that you can edit your notebooks whenever you need to without much hassle.

To dock One Note to your desktop, all you have to do is click on the view tab and click on the Dock to Desktop option and the app will automatically dock itself to the desktop below all the other open windows. Other windows may move a little, but you will always be able to see all the information displayed in them, as well as the information displayed in One Note. However, it must be noted that this feature works best if you have a large monitor screen as resizing the windows may make text hard to read.

10. Creating Outlook Tasks in One Note

One of the most useful features of One Note is the ability to create Outlook tasks that can then be modified at a later date. These tasks are created and edited via a drop-down menu in One Note. The menu has a range of options that include options to delete or open a task in Microsoft Outlook. The tasks that you create will add themselves to your Outlook automatically as long as you have set up and configured the application on the same computer that you are using One Note on.

It is important to remember that you do not have to create a new task then add the task information to it. It is much simpler to choose an existing item and then select an option from the drop-down menu that is displayed on the screen. Once you have selected the appropriate option, the item will immediately be made a task.

Conclusion

OneNote is one of the most versatile note taking applications on the planet, and is well suited for a wide variety of people from doctors and lawyers to students and researchers, to those people who just love to write things everywhere so that they will not forget them.

If you are one of those people who has never experienced a program or application like this then be warned, this program is addictive. The countless features and endless possibilities will keep you staring at the screen for hours, regardless of whether you are using your smartphone, laptop or PC.

The way it integrates seamlessly with the other programs in the Microsoft Office Suite is also very impressive and is something that you will soon be taking for granted once you get comfortable using the program.

Though OneNote is defined as a free-form information gathering computer program, it is way more than that. It is an organizer, a spreadsheet application, a database management system, a word processor, and countless other things rolled into one.

Although it is not geared towards publishing work, because it integrates so well with the rest of Microsoft Office you do not really need to worry about that. What you do need to pay attention to is the fact that it will make doing your work much easier, and when you feel you have done enough to publish it, you can just transfer it to one of the other programs in the Office Suite to polish it off before releasing it to the world.

This manual has given you a peek into the world that is OneNote. It is a world that is ever changing and full of possibility, and if you choose to enter it, you will never be disappointed.

Organization
The Art of Clean

Organizing Techniques and Stress-Free Life Management

Contents

Introduction

Organization – this is a word that you may hear quite often, but one which could leave you challenged, wondering how you can achieve organization. If you look at your life, you will find that there are periods of stress that you have experienced quite often. Look a little deeper and it is quite possible that you can link these periods to some disorganization, in an area of your life.

When you are disorganized, it means that there is something that is not quite right, which could be that something is out of place, or you are avoiding getting something done which is throwing you off balance. Either way, to enjoy a life that is completely stress free, you will need to get rid of any disorganization in your life, and focus on getting everything that you need in order. This is the book that will help you accomplish this and more.

To begin with, you need to understand the importance of cleanliness, and how a clean environment can be of great advantage to you and what you may be facing. In addition, you will need to be armed with practical and applicable techniques to help you conquer getting organized. In addition, you should consider what it means to have a life that is free of stress, and how you can achieve this by getting yourself organized as quickly as possible.

You can pick up some fail free techniques for all this within minutes, just read on and lean how you can improve your life now.

Chapter 1:
Basic Quick Clean Techniques

Put on your television, and sit down to watch for a short while. On any TV station that you put on, within a short period of time you will view a cleaning advertisement, letting you know of the latest and greatest tool on the market to help you achieve a clean space. Why is this vital to understand? Well, most people realize that if they want to get the best out of any space, and subsequently have a positive interaction or experience within that space, the area needs to be clean.

Cleanliness is the first milestone that you need to overcome when you are looking to get organized. So what exactly is cleanliness? Being clean means that you have taken the time to remove existing dirt that can be seen, and possibly even taken the extra step to help get rid of dirt that cannot be seen.

When it comes to managing your life so that you can maintain a clean space for the long term, there are some things that you can begin to do. The techniques of clean that will help you include the following: -

- **Start at the bottom** – So you need to clean an entire room or a house, and you are at the point where you are wondering where you need to start. Start at the bottom, which means that the first place you need to clean up is the floor. The reason is simple, and that reason is that dirt will rise and settle on surfaces after you sweep something to prepare for mopping or polishing. This dust will need to be cleaned up later, but a surface first means that you will need to go over it again if you want to ensure that it remains clean. The way that you choose to clean a floor depends highly on the type of floor that you are cleaning. Most floors can be swept clean, and then wiped clean using a mop. In the other hand, floors which are made of wood need a different approach, where they are polished after they have been swept clean.

- **Clean up the Surfaces** – Once you have sorted out the bottom within a room, the next place that you need to clean is the surfaces. This is often best done by taking down any little trinkets and ensuring that they have been completely wiped clean. Once they are wiped clean, you need to take some time to polish them up so that they are presentable at their best. Then, you need to wipe down the table top, ledge, or other area that they had been placed on. You can only achieve proper organization when your space is clean, and when you have wiped clean a surface, it becomes easier to strategically arrange your trinkets, keeping you organized.

- **Polish Windows and Glass** – After you have cleaned and arranged your trinkets and other items, it is essential that you clean the windows or any other glassware that could be within the room. There is a natural reaction that people will have towards spaces like these that are clean and shiny. They speak that one is organized, due to their high polished look. They also make it easier for one to get organized, as there is minimal worry about hygiene and cleanliness.

- **Take proper care of pets** - A great contributor to the dirt that shows up in many homes is a pet, in the form of a dog, cat or other furry animals. These animals have the tendency to shed their fur, leading to it clogging in areas around the home. This can be unsightly as well as causing one to experience stress which affects ability to be organized. Pets need to be given the proper care, to prevent them from being a nuisance unintentionally.

The Right Tools

In order for you to get organized by starting off with cleaning, you need to make sure that you are using the right tools for the job. This will mean that you are able to be efficient and get the job done quickly, and in the best way possible. The tools that you need include the following: -

Microfiber Cloth

This is an excellent cloth for cleaning all types of surfaces as it has the ability to easily pick up dust that may have gathered.

Cotton Gloves

These should be plastic on the outside, but have cotton where your skin makes contact with the gloves, to ensure that your skin is able to breathe. These will protect you from injury or causing damage to your hands in the course of cleaning.

Sponge

When you need to clean up a large area, you may need to ensure that you can give it a good scrubbing. The sponges will help to quickly absorb things from the ground, to ensure an excellent clean.

Vacuum Cleaner with Dusting Attachment

Vacuum cleaners are important, especially when you are trying to get rid of dust around the house. They are especially useful when you are trying to eliminate dust from corners, walls and high ceilings.

All Purpose Cleaner

There is no escaping the fact that all the surfaces in our homes will get dirty at one point or another. The best way to get rid of all the smudges, stains, spills and sticky spots is with a good all-purpose cleaner. However, you may also want to invest in an additional cleaners such as an oven cleaner and a glass cleaner for some of the more sensitive surfaces.

Broom and Dustpan

The floors of your home carry nearly all the dirt that comes into your home. Additionally, almost all spillages end up on the floor at some point. For this reason, it is important that you invest in a good broom and dustpan, especially if you do not have a vacuum cleaner. However, before you buy your broom or dustpan, you must consider the type of floor that you have in your home as it could dictate the type of broom that you buy.

Mop and Mop Bucket

Investing in a mop and bucket is as important as investing in a broom and dustpan, especially when you need to clean up liquids from your floor. However, just like with the broom, you are going to have to consider the type of floor that you have before you make your purchase.

Squeegee

Squeegees may not seem like a necessity in your home, but once you invest in one you will understand just how invaluable these little tools can be. They can be used everywhere, from the floors, especially in the bathroom and shower, to the windows.

Scrub Brush

Scrub brushes are especially important in for those areas where a microfiber cloth or sponge will not work. They are particularly good of getting stubborn stains off surfaces around the house.

Toothbrush

Many people do not think about toothbrushes as cleaning tools but they do an excellent job when you need something a little more detailed than a scrub brush. Next time, rather than throwing away all of your old toothbrushes, you should disinfect one or two and use them to help clean the grout, sinks and hard to reach places around the house.

Cleaning a space is an art, as it cannot be gone into blindly. From the points above, it is easy to realize that you need to have a detailed plan of what you are going to clean and how you are going to clean it. Once accomplished, you will find that you experience peace of mind, which can even shift something in the physical aspects of your life.

Chapter 2:
Getting Rid of Clutter

Perhaps the most essential organization technique that you need to master is the ability to get rid of clutter. There are television shows in recent years that have tried to help people understand how clutter can lead to organization, and this ruin your life. Clutter simply refers to items that you have accumulated over an extensive period of time, most of which you are unlikely to use, and also, those which do not add any value to your home. The problem with clutter is that people attach emotional values to an item, making it much more important than it actually is. By hanging on to an item that you do not need, you are adding to the overall stress that you can experience from things piling up, as well as affecting the aesthetic appeal of your space.

There are some questions that you need to ask yourself when you are getting rid of your clutter. These are as follows: -

Is it functional?

Take a critical look at the item that you are holding on to, and that you want to keep. Consider whether it is functional or not. This means that you should be able to put it to good use if necessary, without needing to take it to a repair shop or work on it yourself, and without tampering or altering it in any way. One reason that you could be disorganized is because you are hanging on to items that you hope you will be able to use one day. These are the items which have no value until you have changed the way that they are at the time. So, if you have a broken radio that only needs someone to fix it, and it hasn't been fixed within two weeks of losing functionality, then that item should be considered clutter and disposed of appropriately.

Can I sell it or donate it?

Most people feel awful throwing things out, because they do not believe that things should go to waste. However, if you change your mind set about this, you will find that it is easier to get organized. Rather than worry about where you are going to throw something, especially if it is a large item, or how you will lose out when getting rid of something, think instead about recovering some of your investment through selling the item, or donating the item so that it can be of benefit to someone with greater need. Knowing that you once precious item (which is now clutter) has the chance to bring joy into the life of another person will make it easier for you to get rid of it when the time calls for such action.

Does it add to my happiness?

Why are you really holding on to something? Is it because someone gave it to you once and therefore you consider it to be special? Do you think that you will never find the same item again? When you are looking to get organized by decluttering, you will need to deal with the physical presentation of things that are right in front of you, as well as the emotions that are attached to your property. You will find that items which add to your clutter situation rarely add to your happiness. Therefore, if you want to get rid of something, even though it had been a gift, you should do so to experience organization and a life without stress.

When was the last time I used it?

Do you still have the pen that you used to sign your high school yearbook fifteen years ago? Although you may be hanging onto some property because you believe that it has some sentimental value, doing so is simply a way that you can also add on to the clutter within your home. When you are looking to get organized by getting rid of your clutter, look at an item and ask yourself honestly when you last used the item. The next thing that you need to do is get rid of the item, especially if it has been a month and you have not used it for anything at all. Clutter and sentimentality do not go hand in hand, so if you want to have an exciting life that is organized, you will have to let some things go.

How much is this worth?

Some people end up with clutter because they believe that the property they own will increase in price over time. This is a sound argument to keep something, but that is only if you are keeping one or two items. Clutter becomes evident when a person is hanging on to many things with the belief that over time, they will increase in value. It would be better to sell these items when possible, rather than hope that things will remain the same and you could get a better chance of benefitting from increased organization.

How long will I miss it once it is gone?

Out of sight in many cases is out of mind, so when you get rid of an item, you will find that you can forget about that item within a limited period of time. If you find this hard to believe and you are in a cluttered situation, consider this. The item that you want to get rid of, when was the last time that you thought about it. Is it something that you suddenly found that helped the memories rush back? If this is the case, then you can get rid of it as memories flooding you means that you have been able to exist without the item and therefore have no real need for it.

Am I ready for something new?

The reason that many people choose to get organized is because they are ready for a change in their lives, and are willing to welcome something new to their way of functioning and being. If you are ready for something new, then you should seriously consider decluttering. The thing about life is that you need to put something out to get something back in, and the same applies for your clutter. If you are hoping to purchase a new couch, there is no way that you will be able to do so without getting rid of the old one, and creating some space for the new one. When you are decluttering, to ensure that it is now a challenging and emotional situation, just pay attention to the bigger picture and you will find that the entire process is much easier to handle.

Getting rid of clutter means that you are willing to move with the current trends and live a more minimalist lifestyle. This will give you a considerable amount of pleasure, as you will find that you experience peace of mind, with less worries about cleaning up spaces and keeping things in order. It will also become much easier to find the things that you need, as there will be less to look through and everything shall have its pace. This is possible once you get rid of all the clutter, the things that are holding you down and stopping you from achieving the dream of life management, stress free. When you are getting organized, you will discover that you can be much more successful if you only keep what you need.

Chapter 3:
Keeping out the Clutter

When it comes to decluttering your home, it can be really hard to decide what needs to stay and what needs to go, and most importantly, you can begin to lose morale when it comes to picking some items to throw out, especially those that hold sentimental value for you. For this reason, one of the most important things you can do when you begin decluttering is to enlist an anticlutter partner. This will be someone who ensures that you do not lose interest in what you are doing, and that you actually finish the decluttering process. There are a couple of things that you could do with your anti-clutter partner to ensure that the process runs smoother:

- Ensure that you have a time limit for the amount of time you will work, and choose the area you shall be working on and stick to it. If you complete one area before your time is up, you should move on to the next area and continue until you run out of time

- Ensure that you work systematically, for instance, start cleaning from top to bottom, or from one corner of the room to the other

- Make plans to do something with your partner when you are done. You could go out for lunch or a cup of coffee. This will help keep up morale as you will have something to look forward to after the work is done.

Once you have decluttered your space, you are going to need to keep the clutter out of the spaces you have organized. This may seem simple, but it is more challenging than many people would like to admit. Listed below are some steps you can take to stop the clutter taking over your life:

- Start following the "one in, one out" rule. This means that if you buy a new pair of shoes, then you should get rid of an old one that you do not wear any more. Keeping something just in case you need it again is one of the reasons clutter builds up in people's homes

- Keep a bag in your closet for things that you would like to donate, and fill that bag with items that you no longer use or do not have a use for anymore. When the bag is full, you could take it to your local donation center or homeless shelter.

- Place baskets in a central location such as the top of the stairs or main corridor and let them accumulate items you cannot put away instead of leaving things where they do not belong. You can then put the items where they belong at the end of the week or when the basket is full

- Try to dedicate Sunday evening to cleaning up the clutter that has accumulated during the weekend, as there is nothing worse than waking up on Monday morning and realizing that your house is still a mess. Try to recruit as many family members as possible to help you. With younger members, you could make it a game, and give them certain rewards if they manage to complete certain tasks in a given time. Begin by getting everyone to go around the house and identifying what tasks need to be completed, and write them down. Once you have compiled the list, assign different people different tasks and give them a time limit for their conclusion.

- Try to leave every room you enter neater than you found it. If it is the kitchen, make sure that everything is clean after dinner and ready for breakfast the next day. If you have been watching TV, make sure that you put magazines and books away, and rearrange pillows or cushions before you leave the room.

By incorporating these things into your routine, you will be surprised at just how hard it is for clutter to build up in the home. Even if the clutter does build up, it will be for a few hours, not a few weeks.

Chapter 4:
Making Chores easy

Nowhere in the world will you find someone who claims to have the perfect home. However, you can strive to come as close to perfect as possible by ensuring that certain things become a part of your daily routine. For instance, there are some daily chores that can be made so much simpler if they become a part of your routine. This chapter will focus on how you can make certain chores routine, making the cleaning process easier and ensuring that you live in an organized, pleasant environment without spending too much time cleaning.

The Daily Routine

One of the best things you can do for yourself is develop a daily cleaning routine that is both simple and quick, and ensures that everything stays relatively clean.

1. **Make your bed immediately you wake up** – making your bed immediately you get out of it will ensure that you have one less chore to do for the rest of the day

2. **Keep cleaning materials under the sink in the bathroom** – thirty seconds is all you need after washing in the morning to clean up after yourself. You will need to do less major cleaning in the bathroom if you do more minor cleaning like wiping down the sink when you are done using it

3. **Clean up spills when they happen** – whether in the kitchen or the living room, when something spills, clean it up immediately. It may slow you down a little, especially in

the morning, but you will be happy that you do not have to clean anything when it has had time to dry and harden

4. **Minimize the dirt that comes into your home** – you can do this by insisting people take their shoes off when they enter your home, and cleaning the garage at least once a week. Remember, the less dirt you allow in, the time you are going to spend getting dirt out.

5. **Take 5 to 10 minutes each evening to straighten up the house before you sleep** – picking up after yourself just before you sleep will help to drastically reduce the amount of clutter that accumulates in your home. You will also find that as the week progresses, you will have less to pick up. Children should also be taught to do this every day.

Finding the time to clean

There are many of us who would love to have a maid who we could leave to worry about the cleaning. However, unless you can afford it, you will probably have to clean up after yourself. Listed below are a couple of things you can do to help schedule cleaning time without making cleaning a major part of your life.

1. **Plan to do housework** – there are those that use Saturday mornings to do chores and run errands, while there are those who would rather use Sunday afternoons. Whatever the case may be, you need to identify what chores need to be done weekly, write them down, and specify the time frame that you will need to complete them.

2. **If you do not like it, do not clean it** – go through each room and discard anything that you have lost interest in,

such as the potted plant that you were given at your old job, or that present you were given by your secret Santa that has lost its charm.

3. **Time yourself** – measuring how much time it takes to complete certain chores will help you plan better in the future. If you know it will take you about 10 minutes to put the washing in the dryer and start it up, then you will be able to do that the next time you have 10 minutes free.

4. **Invest in a hand vacuum** – these can be very useful for those quick tasks like cleaning up cereal spillage or quickly dusting counter tops and shelves. If you can take care of the chore quickly, you will find it much easier to do

5. **Multitask while you are on the phone n-** if you receive a phone call and you notice that you can do something to clean up while you are talking then do just that. If you can clean out a drawer or do some ironing while you are on the phone then you should, rather than using the time solely for the conversation you are having. Doing this may also help you complete the chore faster.

6. **Consider that some chores can double as exercise** – if you have to vacuum the house or clean out the garage, you should try and see this as an excuse to get some exercise in, and maybe even take a break from the gym that day as you should have already done enough exercise.

7. **Have guests** – when you entertain people, it gives you more motivation to clean up the house, after all, no one wants to have guests come to a dirty house. Not only will you have fun doing it, but if you do it right, you may find that you have even less cleaning to do after the party then before. You should start cleaning up a couple of days before

the party to ensure that you are not completely exhausted the night of the party.

8. **Clean reasonably** – there is no rule out there that says that you have to clean your bookshelves or cabinets every week. Therefore, you should clean your home well enough and consider hiring a company to come do some deep cleaning twice or three times a year.

Share the responsibility and save time

For centuries women have been responsible for the chores around the house. Even in the modern era when many women are working away from home, they are still expected to do most of the house work. Recent statistics reveal that though men today help more than their fathers did, they still do only 15% of the laundry and one-third of the shopping. However, unless a woman lives by herself, there is no reason why she cannot expect or receive help from her significant other. After all, the couple that works together smiles together.

As far as children are concerned, household chores help to teach them to be more responsible. Parents today have to work so much harder to provide the same things for their kids that their parents provided for them, making it harder for them to do some of the household chores. Expecting help from the children should be seen as a fair trade. They should be reminded that by helping out around the house, they could be helping to free time for that family bike ride, or that trip to the zoo.

There are many ways that chores can be shared out. For instance, they can be delegated based on talent, interest, time of completion or even priorities. For this reason, you should develop a way to delegate chores that works for everyone. Developing a system that works is as easy as following the guidelines listed below.

1. **Agree on a goal** – set standards for the home and ensure that everyone understands what the standards are for different rooms. For instance, if you want the beds made in a certain way, make sure that everyone knows this so that they can do it themselves. If you must, demonstrate what you need to be done and how you would like it to be done to make the point clearer.

2. **Let everyone have a say in the chores that they do** – as everyone has their own preferences, they should also have a say in the things that they want to get done. For instance, if you work at night, then maybe you should be the one to take out the trash the night before it is meant to be picked up on your way to work. If you have a child who enjoys cooking, perhaps you could designate a day or two in the week when they cook dinner.

3. **Demonstrate how the chore should be carried out** – regardless of the person, whether they are your child or your significant other, you will need to demonstrate what you need done, especially for those chores where you know the person meant to do it has no clue. For instance, if your spouse is supposed to do the groceries but they have no idea how to make a list, show them how the first time so that they know what it is you would like to achieve.

4. **Create a schedule** – this will allow everyone to know when they need to carry out a particular chore. The schedule can be daily, weekly, or monthly, or even all three. This strategy works especially well with children who

respond well to chore charts, especially when there are rewards that can be gained and marked on the chart.

5. **Ensure that the chores are done regularly** – there are those people who like to do chores when they are in the mood. However, this does not work for all chores, therefore, it is important that you insist that the chores are done according to the schedule you have created

6. **Trade chores every once in a while** – come up with a program where you trade chores with your partner or kids occasionally. It could be every two weeks or every month. Doing this ensures that everyone learns what is needed around the house.

7. **Synchronize your household, especially for major cleanings** – some people prefer to do some chores as a family, especially when it comes to major clean ups. For instance, if you would like to clean the whole house in one afternoon, it may be a good idea to assign different rooms to different members of your family. For instance, you could clean the kitchen and bathrooms while your spouse cleans the living room and your bedroom, and the kids could clean their rooms and the dining room

8. **Get your family to work as a team** – in much the same way some households and offices where someone pays a small fine every time they use a swear word, so too should you have a "mess jar" where members of the family are fined for leaving rooms messy. The person who has the smallest fine at the end of the month can then be rewarded with a week off their chores.

9. **Identify problem areas** – if you find yourself always picking up the slack in certain areas, speak up and let your

concerns be known. If they do not seem to understand what it is you are trying to get them to do, you should steer them towards another chore that you think they will be able to carry out with better results. However, you should not take over what they are doing because you feel they are not doing it properly.

10. **Ensure that you praise a job well done** – nothing works quite as well as praise when it comes to raising morale. Even if the job is not done properly, if effort has been put into it then praise is warranted. You must remember that though you may have high standards, you may have to compromise every once in a while, especially with children.

Chapter 5:
Making Use of Storage Containers

With all your clutter gone, you will be left with the information that you really need, and this is where you get to the heart of organization. These items or information need to be arranged in such a way that they are easy to find when necessary. The best way that you can do this is by using storage containers.

When most people think about storage containers, what comes to mind is those things that are used to keep food within a fridge or a freezer, so that it does not go bad too quickly. However, there are so many other ways that you can use storage containers, and these include the following: -

Kitchen Storage

Making use of containers is an excellent way to keep your kitchen organized. As a technique, you will find that it is flawless both for large items and small items. You will need to have storage containers (the size that you need) as well as labels and a marker. An excellent rule of thumb to remember is that all the storage containers need to have lids, to ensure that what you are storing does not in any way get damaged. The things that you can put within the storage containers include items that you will use on a daily basis, such as flour, sugar, corn flour and so on. It is always advisable to store all the dry ingredients within the storage containers. These would also include flavorings such as dried herbs and spices. Make sure that each container has a label, with what is within it written out in a marker so that you are not constantly opening the containers to assess what could be on the inside.

Garage Storage

The garage is a room that often turns into a dumping ground, where the things that you do not need access to on a daily basis end up being stored and piling up. However, what often happens is that the day you need an item, it becomes almost impossible to find as it seems as though it has been buried under the rubble. This is where organization using garage storage boxes becomes an excellent technique. All that you need to do is create categories for all your property, such that you can put all the tools into one storage container, then old items within another one and so on. Depending on what your garage holds, you can create more intricate categories. This helps with organization as when you are looking for something, all that you will need to do is find a label on a box, and all that is needed would be there.

Special Events Storage

Christmas comes around once in a year. As does Easter, and Halloween. These are holidays which are often lavishly experienced and spent on. There is one minor problem. Following the holiday, one may choose to simply discard of all the décor that they were using, so that they can make space for deco in the coming year. This is all an addition to costs. Instead of choosing this route, it is possible to make use of special events storage containers where you can store items such as Christmas lights and gifts, what you need for the Easter egg hunt and so on.

Wardrobe Storage

There are many different items that you will find in a typical wardrobe. There are items such as dresses and jackets which are typically put on hangers, and then there are skirts, shirts, dresses and so on. When it comes to storage, you can put in all the different items that do not go on hangers into a wardrobe storage box that is labeled for ease of access. These can then be arranged high up in your wardrobe, making sure that you are making the best use of space that you can.

Division of Items Storage

Over the years, you will accumulate a range of different items. These could include items such as books, clothing, ornaments and so on. When you need to put them away, you will need to ensure that there is some order to them, so that you can also retrieve them with ease. Therefore, if you are putting away a dining set, it would be ideal that you place the tablecloth and napkins in one storage bin, with the cutlery and crockery in another. By choosing not to mix up all the items, you are also ensuring that they are stored in a safe way, and that they can be retrieved in a safe way.

Types of Storage Containers

The type of storage box that you choose to use is also important, if you are hoping to get to final organization. The first characteristic that the box should have is that it should be transparent. This makes it easier to see what is within the box without having to worry about constantly pulling it down or taking it off a shelf.

In addition, you should make sure that the storage containers you are using are made of strong plastic. This will make them highly durable, so you will not need to worry about constant replacements with them. However, if you are looking to match the storage containers with the décor within your home, you will find that these containers are made from a range of materials. The materials include cloth, wood, bamboo, raffia, metal and so on. They should also contain lids, no matter what material that they have been made from. When they have lids, it is easier to stack them one on top of the other to better maximize space.

The shape of the containers can also help you with getting organized. Containers that are square or rectangular in shape are typically easier to use for storage than those which are circular in shape. Remember, you can choose to get them in different sizes to suit what you wish to be stored within them.

If you interact with any professional organizer, you will notice that they are always advocating for the use of storage containers, and the reason for this is that when you use them, they work incredibly. Having a container for everything in your home means that you ensure there is a place for everything, and you do not have items simple scattered around. This is key in organization, as one of the primary rules is that you need to put things back. With storage containers, you known where you need to put them back.

The Rules of Placement

Having storage to be able to put your stuff in is one thing, however, knowing where to put it once you have stored it properly is a whole other ball game. Ensuring that everything that you need is easy to find can actually be more challenging than you think. However, there are a couple of things that you can do to help you find things easier, and ensure that you never have to look more than a minute for what you are looking for.

1. **Keep it near where you use it**

When you are arranging your rooms, ensure that you keep stuff near within a few steps of where it is needed. For instance, in the dining room, make sure you store your mats in a cabinet near the table, pens and pads should be kept together on desks and counter tops, umbrellas and boots should be kept near the door and your linen closets should be near a bedroom.

2. **Store items according to how often you use them**

When you are re-arranging your rooms, you should keep in mind how often you use certain items. Those that are not used regularly should be kept out of the way, while items you use every day should be within easy reach. For instance, cups and plates should be stored in cabinets that are around eye level, while things such as holiday decorations can be placed in cupboards high above you or even in the basement or garage.

3. **If you don't use it often, rent it don't buy it**

There are certain things that we own that we only use once or twice a year. Things like camping tents and garden tillers that are used rarely can be rented rather than bought. This will not only help you save on space, it will also help you save on things like maintenance costs.

4. **Designate specific places for incoming and outgoing items**

Every household has things that are either coming in or going out at any given point in time. There may be new purchases that have just been made, or you may have to take your laundry to the drycleaner. By designating specific areas in your home for these items, you will help save on space and ensure that you avoid creating clutter.

Chapter 6:
Organizing the Rooms of your Home

Storing things properly is only the tip of the iceberg when it comes to organizing your home and reducing clutter. Sometimes storing things properly leads to a situation where the rooms in your house start to seem that they are not "lived in" because they seem too sterile. However, there is a fine line between "lived in" and messy, and staying on the right side of that line can be tricky. There are a couple of strategies that you could use to ensure that your rooms stay clean and tidy but also look habitable.

For instance, you could keep a shelf or box underneath the coffee table to ensure that you have easy access to storage for newspapers and magazines. You could also make use of baskets to store toys that are too bulky or large to put in drawers or on shelves. If you allow snacking or eating in the living room, make sure all your family members get into the habit of clearing up after themselves immediately they are done.

Listed below are the different areas in the home that get cluttered the most, and some things you can do to stop the build-up of clutter in those areas.

1. The bathroom

- If you have the space to do so, put shelves and cabinets on the walls and store as much as you can in those spaces rather than on the counter

- Make use of small baskets to help you group and hold related items like makeup and cleaning products

- Ensure that the items that you use in the shower and bath are in a shower caddy

- Use mesh bags to store bath toys

- Store extra rolls of toilet paper close to the toilet. You could store them in a cabinet or a basket on the back of the toilet, or even hanging on the wall.

2. The hall closet

- Hang coats according to length and season as this will allow you to create floor storage. Also, you could double hang in some parts of the closet to save on space

- Hang your children's coats and accessories at their height on the door of the closet

- Arrange the adult's gloves, scarves, purses, etc. in bins or baskets on the shelves in the closet

- Keep boots in containers or boxes so that they stay in place

- Make use of pegs and hooks to hang umbrellas, scarves and flashlights.

3. The Linen Closet

- Make sure that the sheets you buy for each bed are different colors so that you can easily identify the sheets you need when you need them. This should also apply to sheets of different sizes.

- Fold sheets in pairs, with the pillowcases tucked in the middle

- Sort towels into sizes, owners, and color. Place towels that are not used often such as beach towels on a shelf that is hard to access

- Find alternative uses for worn towels, such as washing the car or pets, or get rid of them all together

- Large items like the vacuum should be placed on the closet floor

4. The clothes closet

- If you can, double hang some of your outfits

- Make sure all the hangers are facing in the same direction to stop them getting tangled

- Ensure that you keep your outfits together. This will help you save time when you are picking clothes, and help reduce the stress of finding something that matches

- Keep scarves on hangers to save space

- Invest in a hat box and shoe rack. Hat boxes are especially useful for storing bathing suits, belts, handbags and things such as handkerchiefs and eyeglass cases.

- Store bulky items such as winter jackets and sweaters in containers underneath the bed when it is warm

- Sort through your clothes at the end of each season and discard clothes that you do not need anymore

- Ensure that you set aside clothing that needs to be cleaned instead of throwing dirty clothes back into your closet.

5. Jewelry

- While sorting through your jewelry, you will inevitably find pieces that you didn't even remember you had. Ensure that you rid yourself of jewelry that you will never use again to cut down on the clutter in your jewelry box.

- Get rid of worn or broken items, as well as things like earrings with missing partners.

- Once you have completed clearing the clutter from your jewelry box, arrange it in order of the items that you use the most, making sure that these items are in easier reach than items that you wear rarely.

- If you do not have a jewelry box with sections, get one. This will make it even easier to find what you need to when you need it.

- Make use of jewelry stands and hooks to hang some of your jewelry. You could also use hooks on walls to hang your necklaces. This not only allows you to see what you have, but if done properly it can also work to enhance the art around the house.

6. The Night Table

- Make sure that the things that you are storing on your bedside table are useful to you. Get rid of the books that you have never gotten round to reading and the year old magazines by either finding somewhere else to store them or by donating them.

- Keep only the necessary things on your bedside table, such as tissues, a flashlight, lip balm, a book or two, and an alarm clock, find alternate storage for everything non-essential.

7. Books

- Save time by presorting your books. This will ensure that you do not have to organize books that you are not going to use or that you do not want to keep. Go round the house picking books that you know you are not going to read off shelves, and you will be surprised how much space you can clear. Donate the unwanted books to charities, schools, hospitals or libraries.

- Calculate how much space you will have to store your books, then calculate the amount of space you need to store the books you have chosen, and plan accordingly so that you can either create more space for the books you need or get rid of some books so that they fit in the available space.

- Turn unused space in your home into bookshelves if you can, and if you cannot, invest in bookends so that you can store your books on tables or desks, not just in bookcases

- Try and arrange your books according to different categories like in a library, for instance, science fiction and fantasy books should be together, while non-fiction books and autobiographies can occupy the same space.

- Try not to pack the shelves too tightly or else you will not be able to access the books you need quickly

- Do not store your books in two rows, ensure that they are all in one row to make finding what you need easier

- Allocate a reading shelf for books that you are considering reading next. This will ensure that you will be able to find your next book quickly.

Chapter 7:
Organization and Stress Relief

There is a direct link between being organized and experiencing relief from stress, and several angles through which this direct link can be analyzed. To begin with, it comes down to the way that a person handle organization. There are two main factors that need to be taken into consideration when getting organized, and those are planning and prioritizing. With these taken carefully into consideration, one is able to get organized with ease and prevent having to deal with stressful situations.

Planning

Planning basically means bringing the future into the present in order to be able to do something about it at that instant. Planning ahead matters in everything that you approach in life. Proper planning will help you reach your goals faster and to execute any project you might be working on.

Everyone wants to achieve more every day so that in the long run, a person has less to do. However, have you ever asked yourself why this never happens even when you work harder and for longer period of time? Well, when you do not plan, you procrastinate, meaning that you start leaving things to a later date. This often leads to the things piling up until they become more than you are able to handle. Thinking and planning are what opens up your mental power to trigger your creativity as well as increase your mental and physical energy for you to do what you have planned to do.

When you plan for the purpose of organization, you are looking to get total returns out of everything that you invest in planning, which include your mental investments, physical and emotional. Experts say that every minute that one spends in planning results to ten minutes being saved in the execution of the plan. This is what brings satisfaction in one's life.

Reasons why planning ahead is important

- To access opportunities:

Many tasks are left undone a day because of insufficient opportunities to do them. Planning ahead can help you access the available opportunities to determine whether they will be enough for the tasks ahead. If they are not enough, you can always look for an alternative in order to ensure that everything will be done as per the plan. You are able to think of the opportunities and resources to handle different tasks when you are planning to make things easy when the time to execute the plan comes.

- To access risks and difficulties

Risks and difficulties are always there and these can hinder you from performing well. Planning ahead can help you acknowledge these ahead of time so as to make things easier by the time you are working on the plan. Once you get to a certain task, you will already be aware of the possible difficulties that you could face and dealing with them becomes easier.

- To improve performance

There is always a direct correlation between preparation and performance. Prior planning improves performance by a great percentage. Planning helps you see clearly what you are supposed to do next and this improves the overall performance. This works very well in businesses as well. You are likely to face little stress and difficulties when you are working with a plan. People who plan are able to do more and to produce high quality results at all times

- To become proactive

People who do not plan only respond to the challenges that they face in a day but people who plan becomes more proactive and less reactive. This makes it possible for one to take the right course of action in case of challenges and difficulties, with no regrets afterwards. Nothing becomes hard when you have planned well for it. If you want to respond to situations other than react to them, you should always plan ahead.

- There is enough time to develop teams

If you are planning for something that will involve a team, you will have enough time to develop the right teams to ensure that the project will be a success. This is particularly important when your target is organization as you need to ensure that everyone within the team is on the same page of understanding. Without a proper plan, you might pick the wrong people for your team and the team will be confused right from the beginning, without knowing what to do and how to do it. This can lead to wastage of so much time and energy, and also will mean that you do not get the results you were hoping for.

Prioritizing

Prioritizing is very important in organization. Everyone has different kinds of tasks that they have to accomplish every day, and one needs to know how to prioritize to ensure that they can organize their activities as smoothly as possible. There are those that are very important and there are those that are not really important. Prioritizing will help you deal with the most important tasks first, then you can deal with those tasks that are less important as the day progresses. Prioritizing is good because it helps you save time and it can help you reduce your stress levels by a high percentage.

How to prioritize

- Always start with a master list: this is the list that will have all the tasks that are to be done in a day, including the most important and the least important of them all. You should rank the tasks at this stage of planning.

- From the list, pick out those tasks that should be top in the priority list. These should be the tasks that carry serious consequences if they are not done on time. Focus on the consequences in order to determine how important a task is. These can be named the A-level tasks

- Now categorize all the other tasks that will remain in B, C, D and E level categories. The B level tasks are still important but they carry a lesser penalty if they are not finished by the end of the day. The C level tasks on the other hand do not carry any penalty at all. D tasks are for delegation. If you have someone to help you out with those, you can save some time for the A-level tasks. Finally, the E-level tasks are those that can be eliminated. If you do not have enough time for all the tasks, you can do away with these tasks.

This should be done every day of your life if you want to be organized enough to meet all of your goals. Here are important tips that can help you prioritize effectively:

- Always respect deadlines: if some of the tasks you have in your to-do-list have a deadline, you have to give those tasks some urgency to be able to accomplish them before the deadline. For this, you will need to use an organization tool such as a calendar that can show you at a glance what needs to be done. If you are dealing with clients, you have to give them a positive experience when working with you and this is possible if you are able to meet deadlines at all times.

- Work with goals: working with goals ensures that you are working more and enjoying more rewards even before the end of the set period. Set monthly goals for instance and see just how much you can accomplish in a month. You should start by listing some of the things that needs to be done in a month, then you can incorporate simple tasks that needs to be done in a day to ensure that by the end of the month, everything that was to be done has already been done.

- Always set milestone deadlines for every task: this will ensure that they are accomplished on time. Take every task and break it down into different sub-tasks, then set some simple deadlines that each sub-tasks should be accomplished. This makes it easy to finish the entire task on the set time, which in turn helps you to remain more organized with your work.

- Consider the time required to complete a certain task. If you have many tasks on your list of priorities, you should start with those that will take you less amount of time, then you can dedicate enough time for the most demanding tasks.

- Always think of the consequences: this will ensure that you are prioritizing the the art of cleanmost important projects and that you are working on them within the set timelines in order to avoid dealing with the consequences later on.

- Consider the terms of payment as well. Some tasks will not be paid until they are completely done and this means that you have to work hard in order to get the pay. If that is the case, you will put them top in the priority list if you really want to get that pay. Some tasks will not be paid for after the deadline ad this means that you have to finish working on them by the deadline

From this information, it becomes clear that there is so much you can accomplish with stress relief if you take adequate time to plan for what you are doing, and then to prioritize tasks so that the most important are done first. This is all about creating a routine and procedure that works for you, as being organized means that you attain maximum efficiency, and the spillover result is that you feel much better and more confident.

Chapter 8:
Managing Every Area of Your Life

You should have a clear idea of what you can do on the ground to help you get organized starting immediately. All it takes is several small actions and changes in the way that you do things and you will be on the way. This is excellent, because on the outside, it appears that everything is working like clockwork – to perfection. However, on the inside, it becomes clear that you need to manage every area of your life, in order for you to be organized.

Getting organized in this way can be tough, though here are some basic life management skills that you can always try:

1. Identify the four main aspects of your life. These are outlined as the spiritual or personal development aspect, family and relationship aspect, personal care and health aspect and career aspect. These are the areas that your entire life revolves around. You need to know how much time you should give to each of these as they are all important in different ways. The reason for this is so that you get the right balance to help you maintain proper organization. If you give one aspect more attention that it is meant to receive, then you create an imbalance, which often physically manifests as disorganization.

2. Always write things down. Many people rely on their memory for planning as well as executing certain tasks, but this does not really work effectively all the time. You have to write down what you intend to do and how you intend to do it for a plan to work. This is what being organized is all about. The way that you are writing things down is also important, and one tool that you will find very handy is a

checklist. If you rely on your memory too much, you can get stressed out quickly, as you will be burdened with trying to keep track of too much information at one time. With a written plan, prioritizing becomes much easier and you can always say no to any time robbing activity that will come your way.

3. Live in the present, meaning you should only concentrate on what you are doing at that instant. This is a common cause of disorganization, as you could spend too much time focusing on what has happened in the past which means that you miss all the things that are happening in the present. On the other hand, you could be thinking so much of what is to come in the future, that you spend all of your time constantly planning and never actually executing the plan. Either way, you will experience elevated levels of stress. If you are spending some time with your family for instance, worrying about work and meetings will only rob you of the precious time and the fun you should be enjoying with your family at that moment. Worry and not being in the moment only makes your life more dissatisfactory.

4. Always practice mental control to be able to focus on only what is important at that instant. This means that you need to think about what you are paying attention to. Organization is by no means passive, it is highly engaging and active, and calls for one to have the right presence of mind. If you do this and you give sometime to every important aspect in your life, you will never feel as though you are missing out or as though you are losing the reigns of control. You will feel organized.

5. Be patient with yourself. Do not push yourself too hard and always remember that you cannot do everything at once.

Organization is a gradual process that needs to be learned and mastered in order for it to be adequately applied in your life. Love yourself as well so that you will know how to appreciate the little effort that you make every day. This will help you enjoy life much better. When you are in a positive mind frame, and encouraged about what you could achieve, organization becomes so much easier.

Managing your life means that you need to do a critical evaluation of where you are and what you have achieved. You should look at two main points and these are: -

There are things that people need to remember at all times:

- The demands of life will never end. You will always be required to do this or the other that is why learning how to strike a balance in life will help a lot. Do not push itself harder hoping that one day you will be able to get everything done because this will disappoint you so much in the end.

- You have to know what is important in life and what is not really important to be able to know what deserves more of your time than the other.

With these in mind, it will become easier to understand how you can get organized, and what you are actually capable of achieving. Getting organized should not be an uphill task, and knowing what you are able to handle will make it seamless.

Chapter 9:
Conquering Tardiness

When you are first trying to organize your life, you will notice that of all the obstacles you will face, the hardest to conquer are usually tardiness, whether on your part or someone else's,. Overcoming this obstacle is easier than most people think though, and is as simple as following the simple steps that are outlined in this chapter.

Lateness

Lateness is something that is becoming increasingly hard to avoid. While many people think that other people's lateness is a time waster, it is important to remember that your own lateness also helps to waste time. For instance, if you are half way to the airport and you realize that you do not have any photo identification to get you on your flight, or when you make mistakes during a presentation because you decided to rush through its preparation, a lot of the time the reason why you end up forgetting things is because you were late before you were supposed to carry out the task. Conquering lateness will help you live a more relaxed productive life where you will no longer have to worry about being late or not knowing everything in a presentation, and all you have to do is follow these simple steps.

1. Make punctuality a priority

With everything that has been stated above you may find it rather difficult to make punctuality a priority, but if you begin to make punctuality a priority, you will realize that even when other people are late, the fact that you are early and well prepared will reduce your stress levels. Better yet, you will realize that you will have more time to do the things that you feel are important to you.

For instance, if you find yourself meeting a friend who is always late, rather than arriving for the meeting late for the meeting in anticipation of their lateness, why not show up a few minutes early instead, but take something that you have been wanting to do with you. It may be that Sudoku puzzle book that you were given on your birthday that you have never been able to use, or a magazine that you have not been able to read. You could then read the magazine or do a puzzle while you are waiting for your friend, and accomplish something that you have wanted to do that you have not had the time to complete.

2. Prioritize your morning departures

Regardless of who you are or your lifestyle, the one thing that people find difficult is to be on time in the morning. If you are a parent, you are usually leaving with kids, or leaving them behind, whereas if you are single, even though you do not have these added responsibilities the morning departure can still be difficult.

In fact, this process is so challenging for most of us that the New York Times once asked readers to send in stories with reasons why they got to work late. There were a number of generic answers such as traffic congestion and bad weather. However, there were a few interesting answers, such as the lady who had to console her husband because his pet spider had died. This answer just goes to show that it does not really take much to slow you down in the morning. For this reason, it is important to ensure that you prepare yourself for morning the night before, and keep these tips in mind as you do so:

- Ensure that you have picked your outfit for the next day the night before, and if you have kids, make sure that they have done the same. By ensuring that you know what you are going to wear the next day in the evening, you will cut down the time that it takes you to get changed in the morning. Additionally, if the weather takes a turn for the worse (or the better) during the night, then you will find it much easier to modify an outfit that you picked the night before rather than picking a whole new outfit in the morning.

- Ensure that your purse or briefcase have been packed the night before, and that everything that you will need for the next day is inside. This will make it harder for you to forget something in the morning, and you will not have to do a mad dash between your car and the house because you have to keep getting things you have forgotten.

- If you have kids, you should get them to pack their bags the night before as well, that means books that they may need the next day, kit that they may need to carry to school, and homework that they have completed. If possible, get your kids to put their homework back in their bags immediately they complete it.

- Place all the bags that you are going to need in the morning by the door before you go to sleep. This way, you do not have to start looking for bags in the morning, and they are conveniently placed to allow you to pick them up on the way out.

- If you make lunches for your kids, make sure that you make them immediately after dinner.

- If there is just too much to do the night before, write yourself a note and stick it on the fridge or the counter explaining what it is that you need to do in the morning.

- When you wake up in the morning, do not just wander from room to room as you are getting ready, ensure that you have completed all the tasks that you need to in one room before you go to the next. For instance, if you go into the kitchen for breakfast, fix it, eat it, then clean up after yourself before you move on to the next room

- Keep clocks in the bathroom and the bedroom to remind you of the time while you are getting ready

- Confirm your appointments before you leave the house. You may discover that you have some free time due to unforeseen circumstances, and can now plan to do something else.

For those of us who are hopelessly late regardless of what we try, there are a few things that you can do other than the points mentioned above to help you keep time.

- Keep a clock in every room in the house, including the bathroom

- Set your clocks a few minutes ahead, for instance ensure that all the clocks in your home are 10 minutes ahead

- Mark appointments in your planner ahead of schedule

- Keep a kitchen timer in your bathroom and set it for 10 minute intervals to ensure that you do not take too long getting ready.

Chapter 10:
Creating Order without Procrastination

There are many people out there who know some of the best techniques to help them get organized, the only problem is they are always procrastinating. There are many reasons people procrastinate, some of which include:

- The task they are trying to carry out is overwhelming or time consuming

- They do not know where to start

- The suffer from poor work ethic

- They have something more interesting to do

Most of the time, people will wait for the task or job to be done by someone else, or that the need to do it will suddenly disappear. However, under normal circumstances the task still has to be carried out, and therefore procrastination does not really help. There are many ways you can prevent procrastination, some of which are listed below.

1. **Organize yourself accordingly**

Organizing yourself accordingly does not mean doing some cleaning or straightening out your desk, it means literally organizing yourself for the task ahead. For instance, if you are supposed to be starting a new project, ensure that you write a list that outlines the steps that need to be taken to complete the project, and should you need any files or documents, ensure that you have placed them in the same file folder to make it easier to find them. Additionally, it is important to remember that you do not need to have everything fall perfectly into place for you to begin the project.

2. Assess the environment you shall be working in

There are many people who procrastinate because the area which they are supposed to be working in is not conducive for work. Therefore, before you begin working, ensure that things like filing drawers are in order and the files are easy to access. Additionally, when it comes to things like bills, try to ensure that create a common area for them so that when it comes to addressing them you are not scouring the whole house wondering what you did with them.

3. Break down your tasks

If you have an immense task, perhaps you need to come up with a large presentation for work, then one of the best things that you can do to stop yourself from procrastinating is to break down the tasks into small steps. For instance, rather than think of tackling the whole presentation at the same time, break it down into related topics or better yet, work on it slide by slide and you will soon find that it is not that hard to complete.

4. Begin with the hardest task

If you have a packed day, one of the best ways you can stop procrastination is to begin with the hardest task first. That way, the most demoralizing task has been completed early, and you will then have motivation to complete the rest of the tasks you have in front of you.

5. Make appointments with yourself

If you fail to set time aside to do things then you will never get anything done. For instance, if you have thought of growing a garden for years but have never started doing it, it's probably because you neverset an appointment with yourself to do so. You do not have to start with a 1 hour appointment, 5 minutes us enough as a start, and you can begin by using those 5 minutes to collect the materials and tools you will need to continue your project, or even making a phone call to get information about a pending project. The best things about cell phones is that they allow you to communicate with people anywhere, at any time. Therefore, if you are supposed to have an appointment and the person you are meeting is late then you can use the time waiting to make a few calls and still use the otherwise wasted time constructively.

6. Plan your relaxation time and use it for relaxation

Quite a few people these days procrastinate because they feel that they never get time to relax. If you designate time for relaxation, then you will find that you no longer need to play hooky when you are supposed to be working.

Chapter 11:
Creating order by minimizing Interruptions

Though it may not seem like it, for many people one of the reasons why it seems that they can never get anything done is because they are always getting interrupted. For instance, you could be in the middle of a meeting and your cell phone rings, or you could be leaving the house for an appointment and your dog escapes and runs down the street. These may seem like minor interruptions to you, but they can make your brain overload trying to process what you would like it to do AND what is going on around you.

The best thing to do when it comes to interruptions is to stand up for yourself and learn how to take control of the things that interrupt you. There are two ways you can do this:

1. Anticipate the interruptions

2. Shorten the interruptions when they happen

1. Anticipating the Interruptions

Most of the time, the things that end up interrupting you could have been avoided because you could have foreseen them. For instance, if you have a new recruit working under you then you can be certain at some point in the day they will interrupt you. The same thing goes with children and homework, when your kids have homework, more often than not they will ask you for help, especially if they are very young. If you would like to get rid of some of the stress these interruptions can cause, first you have to make some allowances for them. Here are some things you can do to help you cope with them.

1. **Make realistic forecasts about your uninterrupted time**

Many people can only keep about an hour a day to themselves without interruptions, with the lucky few being able to set aside as much as three hours. If you come to terms with the fact that you will be interrupted at some point, then it becomes easier for you to claim a little time as your own

2. **If you can foresee the interruptions, group them together**

When you are at work, try and ensure that all the interruptions that you could go through happen at the same time. For instance, group all your appointments in the morning or in the afternoon. At home, if you know the delivery man is going to bring over a new fridge, try and make sure that he brings it around the same time that your handyman has agreed to come see you.

3. **Act unavailable and watch the interruptions dwindle**

If you want to reduce the number of interruptions you go through every day, one of the best things you can do is make yourself look unavailable. For instance, when you are at the office, try to position your desk in such a way that you do not make eye contact with people as they walk past. When at home, try as much as possible to avoid the areas where you are most likely to be interrupted, such as the kitchen or the Livingroom

4. **Anticipate the outcome of the things that happen around you**

Learning how to read the situations around you will go a long way to helping reduce the number of interruptions you get every day. For instance, if it is raining outside when you wake up in the morning, make sure you get the children's rain coats and umbrellas while you are taking out your own. This ensures that you do not have to do it later, or have to start searching for things just before you leave the house. If your boss goes on holiday, make sure you free yourself on the day that they return so that you be available to update them on everything that happened in their absence.

5. **Tell people when they can call you**

One of the most irritating interruptions right now is our cell phones. There are many times when people call you at inappropriate times, you may be in a meeting, or at a child's birthday party. To minimize the number of interruptions you get from your cell phone, you should designate time blocks that are dedicated to phone calls. For instance, when you are at home, you may decide that the best time to call would be between 7:00 and 9:00 PM, whereas at the office you may decide to dedicate afternoons to receiving phone calls, allowing you to work more peacefully in the morning.

Learning how to manage interruptions

You may try as hard as you like, but there will always be some form of interruption that you cannot prevent. Despite the fact that they are unavoidable, you can manage these interruptions by implementing some of the strategies listed below:

1. **Ensure you are the top priority**

When someone tries to interrupt you, try asking them whether you can talk in a few minutes, or how much time they need. If they need anything more than 5 minutes, ask them whether you can set up an appointment for a later date or time.

2. Learn to be firm

Sometimes the person who is interrupting you will be relentless, either because they don't realize that your busy, or because you are on a break. You need to learn how to tell them "Not now" and give them a rough estimate of when you will be able to attend to them. This works even with children, who you can even get to time you to ensure that you keep up your end of the bargain.

3. Take charge of the situation

There are often times when the person interrupting you will take ages to get to the point. In those circumstances, try to take charge of the situation by asking something like "how can I help you?" to help them get to the point faster.

4. Keep it short

When you get interrupted, try as hard as possible not to allow the interruption to last longer than it should. Try to wrap it up as quickly as possible so that you can go back to what you were doing. Many people let the interruption take over and even encourage the interrupter to stay, rather than ending the interaction as quickly as possible so that they can get back to what they were doing.

5. Find something else to do while you are being interrupted

If you get interrupted in the office by a coworker, you could try doing something while you are chatting with them, like organize your files. At home, when the repair man comes over, rather than watching over him like a hawk you could do some household chores while he works.

6. Involve the person interrupting you

This usually works to your advantage and is a brilliant way of dealing with interruptions. For instance, if you are at work and a coworker interrupts you for a 5 minute chat, why not get them to help you with that presentation for your boss as you catch up? At home, when your kids interrupt you to play, why not get them to help you with the gardening or a few chores instead. They may actually be overjoyed to help you, especially if they are interested in what you are doing.

Minimizing Self-Interruption

One of the biggest obstacles people have to actually creating order in their lives is when they interrupt themselves in the middle of a task. This is happening increasingly more often, especially with the Internet and social media. Self-interruption happens most often when you are trying to avoid something, or when you are being interrupted so much by external forces that you cannot focus on the task at hand anymore.

There are many things that you can do to stop yourself self-interrupting, such as:

1. **Get rid of temptations**

If you have desk work to do, ensure that your desk is clear of anything that may distract you from the task at hand. When you are on the internet, avoid clicking on links that may lead you away from what you are working on.

2. **Ensure you have everything you need with you**

You need to make sure that you have everything you need with you before you get to work. If you are supposed to be packing, make sure that you have all the boxes, tape, storage containers etc. near you so to that you do not have to keep on looking for things. This will not only help stop you from self-interrupting, it will also save you time, and you will be able to work more efficiently.

3. Focus on one thing at a time

Once you have begun a project, make a promise to yourself that you will work on only that project. If it is a large project, remember to break it down into smaller parts as mentioned earlier. This will help you to take small breaks while you are working on the project, and therefore reduce the chances of you self-interrupting. Additionally, you should ensure that you do not start a new project until you have completed the one you are working on.

Chapter 12:
Organizing your Office

So far many of the organizational techniques discussed in this book have dealt with decluttering and organizing your home. Creating order in the workplace may be a little bit trickier, but it will invariably help you free up time for yourself so that you can relax more and relieve yourself of some stress.

There are many offices that are just covered in clutter. This is mostly because the lives we live right now are so fast paced that people have less time to attend to the papers and files that arrive on our desks. However, decluttering your workplace and creating a more streamlined workspace will invariably help you to be more productive, and give you a clearer picture of the projects that are important.

The best way to find out if you have space that is comfortable, convenient and conducive to work is to perform a quick checkup, using the following list as a guideline.

1. Do you get distracted by people walking by your desk or office?

If you get easily distracted by people walking past your desk or office, consider changing the position of your desk. For instance, if your desk faces the door to your office, perhaps you could move it to the center of the room, and keep the door to your side. This way, you will still be able to welcome people to your office, but you will not be distracted by them walking by your door

2. Do you have many visitors?

There may be something about your office that attracts people to it. For instance, if you have a comfortable chair that people love to have an excuse to sit in, you may have to replace it with one that is not so appealing. Try a director's chair, it is comfortable enough for a meeting, but not something that someone will want to sit in for an hour unless it is really important.

3. Do you have to replace your supplies often?

If you have to replace supplies frequently, then you may need to set up a system for yourself. For instance, you could place a clipboard in the cabinet with all your supplies, and have anyone who takes anything out of it note down what they took and that a new one should be ordered. You should then check the list every week to check and see what needs to be replaced. Doing this will ensure that you never run out of supplies when you need them.

4. Are your files within reach when you are at your desk?

Just the same way you keep frequently used items close to you at home, so too should you keep frequently used files close to you in the office. Files that you use often should be kept in the file drawer in your desk, or in a filing cabinet that is in easy reach.

5. Do you have too much paper around you?

If you find that you have too much paper around you, then you need to make time to sort through it and sort it out according to priority. You will find that you do not need to have all your paperwork stacked on your desk, and that you can find other places to store some papers until they need to be addressed. If you were unfortunate enough to inherit someone else's mess, then you can do two things:

- Take the time to get to know the files that were left behind. Someone may come to your office looking for a file you never even knew was in your possession.

- Mark items that need to go into storage, especially if you have an idea of what can be discarded and what needs to be kept. However, if you are new at the job, you may not know exactly what can go and what needs to stay, so you need to ensure that you know what you are doing before you throw away important papers.

6. **Do you have a recycling bin in your office?**

If you do not have one of these you should. As you are clearing out the clutter you are going to be throwing a lot of paper out. It is better to sort it out sooner rather than later.

7. **Do you have shelves?**

If you have shelves in your office, make sure that they are used exclusively for books and binders. There are too many offices where bookshelves become dumping grounds for anything and everything in the office. If you have stacks of papers on your shelves, sort through them and keep the ones that are needed.

8. **What type of lighting are you using?**

For offices that have fluorescent bulbs, you may want to invest in some incandescent lighting on your desk. Having a lamp on your desk will also help you to read and retrieve files faster as you will not have to strain yourself to see what you are doing.

Once you have sorted out your office it is time to tackle your desk. When you are doing this, make sure that you keep the following questions in mind.

1. Do you keep getting distracted by the things on your desk?

2. If you were to go through your in-tray, would you find files and papers that you should have dealt with weeks before?

3. Does it take you more than 5 minutes to find a document that you need or that someone has requested?

4. Do you often forget where you put a particular document?

5. Has your desk been clear of clutter at any time within the last month?

If you can answer yes to any or all of these questions then you need to do some serious decluttering. However, before you do so, you need to decide what you are going to do with the items on your desk.

- **Toss** – you should toss all papers, memos and pieces of mail that should have been attended to but are now too old to be addressed

- **File** – any papers that you need to keep should be placed in their relevant files. This should be easy to do, especially if you followed the advice about putting files in easy reach of your desk

- **Respond** – all mail, documents and memos that need to be responded to should be addressed. You will find that some of them may just need a signature, while others will need more time. For the ones that need more of your attention, you could put these in a pile to address when you have the time, and ensure that you put them down on a to-do list.

The cleanup sessions that you do on your desk should last a maximum of 15 minutes a day, and should be carried out until you have enough space for the following:

- A blotter

- A telephone

- A clock

- A calendar (if you use a desk calendar)

- A pencil holder for your pens, pencils, scissors, ruler and letter opener

- Paper clip holder

- A stapler

- A tape dispenser

These items are the ones you are most likely to use on a daily basis, and therefore should be kept close at hand. Once you have gotten your desk clear, you are going to have to keep it clear. The first thing you should do is create three file folders:

1. **The copy file** – this file should contain all the papers that you need to photocopy. If you cannot delegate the copying process, then you need to create time during the day when it would be most convenient for you to do your copying, preferably when the copy room is empty to minimize interruptions

2. **The enter file** – this file should contain all the information you need to enter into your computer. The easiest way to make use of this folder is to pile up all the things that need to be entered into the system and deal with them at the same time, perhaps towards the end of the work day.

3. **The take home file** – this file should contain all the papers and documents that you need to work on at home or away from the office. Many people like to put these papers straight into their briefcases, while others prefer to let the papers accumulate then pack them at the end of the day. Choose the method that suits you the most.

Once you have decluttered your desk, keeping it neat is quite easy, and is more than possible if you can just follow the three rules listed below.

1. **Keep your desk clean** – the only things that should be on your desk are your accessories and whatever it is you are working on. To achieve this, make sure that you clear your desk every evening before you leave the office.

2. **Address everything that comes into your office the day it arrives** – procrastinating with mail and memos only leads to clutter

3. **Do not keep anything you do not need** – if you have papers or documents that can be stored somewhere else then you should move them to that storage space. Similarly, if you receive work that someone else can handle better than you can, delegate the duty, do not keep the papers floating around your desk so that you can struggle with them later on.

4. **Keep your in-box and out-box off your desk** – this may not seem like it makes sense, as in-boxes and out-boxes can really help you to manage paper flow, but they can end up being a source of clutter on your desk. To stop them becoming a source of desk clutter, you should put them on a credenza or on a shelf or table near the door. This will not only help you keep clutter off your desk, it will also ensure that you do not get distracted by the mounting paperwork , allowing you to work better.

While you are putting some of the steps outlined above into practice, you need to ensure that you also begin changing some of your habit related to work so that you can maintain the order that you have finally achieved. For instance, you need to start assigning a regular time where you will be handling paperwork. Even if it means coming to work an hour early, or staying an extra hour afterwards to clear up the paperwork on your desk, ensure that it becomes a routine so that you can minimize the amount of work you will have to do the next day. Additionally, you need to ensure that you handle all new paperwork that comes to your desk quickly and efficiently, and remember to refile any papers that you may have taken out of their files.

Creating order within your files

This chapter has talked a lot about files and ways in which you can order them to be able to reduce the clutter in your office. There are additional strategies that you can use to help you minimize the chaos that can come from having too many papers in the office.

1. Process everything that comes across your desk completely. If you cannot answer a letter or email, make sure that you

make notes on it and place it in a separate file of documents to be addressed later. The notes will help you because you will not have to reread the document when you get back to it

2. Create an under five minutes folder for all those tasks that can be addressed in under five minutes. This folder should be used when you have a little spare time but cannot start a large task immediately, such as when you are just about to go for lunch, or when you are waiting for a meeting to start.

3. Make sure that you file everything at the end of the day. Ensuring that all your papers are in relevant files will not take long, especially if you get into the habit of doing it every day. It should not take you more than an hour in the beginning, but as time passes and you get more things in order you should see that time come down to no more than 15 or 20 minutes at the end of your work day.

Doing this does not only help you save time filing in the long run, it also helps you keep track of where everything is, and saves you time when it comes to searching for documents at a later date.

The easiest way to tell if you have gotten it right is by trying to access a file that you stored away. If you can access a document that you filed away in under three minutes then you have a good filing system. If it takes you longer than that then you need to rearrange your filing system.

Conclusion

Every day, there are a myriad of things that you need to accomplish. In order to get things done in the most efficient way, you will need to have the help of specialized tools and techniques. The techniques within this book address the way that you are managing your life, particularly when it comes to your ability to be organized. It is through organization, that you will find it possible to enjoy every moment of your life.

It is essential that you think about what it means to really enjoy your life. In a nutshell, to live a stress free life, you need to strike a balance between what you have to do and what you need to do. The problem is that many people do not really know how to balance their lives. For this very reason, you should learn how to organize your life so that you will cater for all the things that you have to do so that you are able to set time aside for recreation and relaxation.

Time management is essential as with only a few hours in a day, you should be able to plan for every minute so that you satisfied with what you have been able to achieve. This is what will motivate you to do more each day.

Stress free life management entails a lot, and with this book as your guide, you have all the information that you need to have an easy and fulfilling life, that is completely stress free. You now know how to prioritize, to plan, to stay organized and you will find that you attract numerous benefits to your life and well-being.

Manufactured by Amazon.ca
Bolton, ON

18679737R00074